To Margarien
My new friend

LIBERATION
of Mind, Will, and Intellect

Psalm 91

David Keklikian

11-10-2024

All Scripture quotations are taken from the King James Version of the Holy Bible.

Boldface type or italicized references indicate author's emphasis.

Attribution to other authors is given where known. Notification of any omission will initiate a correction.

TITLE Copyright © 2020 by David Keklikian.

Printed in the United States of America

No portion of this book may be used or reproduced by any means: graphic, electronic or mechanical, including photocopying, recording, taping, or by any information storage retrieval system, without the written permission of the publisher, except in the case of brief quotations embodied in critical articles and reviews.

For information contact:
David Keklikian
4612 E 54th St #112
Tulsa, OK 74135

Prepared for Publication By

PUBLISHING

MAKING YOUR BOOK A REALITY

Ceder Point, NC | 843-929-8768 | info@BandBpublishingLLC.com

ISBN: 978-1-0880617-8-7

Limited Promotion Printing: November, 2021

CONTENTS

ACKNOWLEDGMENTS 3
UPFRONT 7
PREFACE 11
CHAPTER ONE 17
Superiority of humans over evil spirits
   Audio-visual deceptions 26
   Demons release body parts 31
   What can believers do? 36

CHAPTER TWO 41
Detailed cases of exorcism
   Demons gang-rape a lady 41
   Stacy and the roaring lion 45
   Lady's face mutates to snarling dog 51
   David of violence 62
   Case of the ebony mask 71
   Psychic chiropractor 74
   Destroyer of relationships 78
   Arlene, Lois and scientology 79
   Case of an orthodox Jew 84
   Case of many voices 90
   Dr. Glen PhD 97
   Inward characteristics 98
   Outward characteristics 98

CHAPTER THREE 101
Mental and physical deliverance

Testimony of Russ Pilcher 103
Author's testimony. 113
Testimony of a lady at seminar. 117
CHAPTER FOUR. 121
Thoughts and imaginations
Meeting the conditions for deliverance 139
Book of the Law 141
Canaan & giants = salvation & demons 144
False gods 146
CHAPTER FIVE. 157
Angels and demons in human affairs
Does evil actually exist?. 158
References to archangel Lucifer 165
Voices of demons 166
Voice of God 166
Dreams, visions, voices, and angels 167
Mental armor. 168
Thoughts and knowledge. 173
How does the devil speak to us?. 176
God's thoughts 181
Man's thoughts 182
How important are your thoughts? 183
Voices. 187
Imaginations: advanced thoughts 190
Fables and fantasies 191
Enhanced thoughts. 192
Mutual heritage. 196
CHAPTER SIX 199
How to keep your deliverance

Hard things 201
Praise and thanksgiving 210
Making notes of self-examination 212

CHAPTER SEVEN **217**
Twenty tips and techniques
Tip 1: Avoiding double jeopardy 219
Tip 2: Nicknames and negative labels 221
Tip 3: Confessing salvation's benefits 225
Tip 4: Humor helps 226
Tip 5: Obey traffic laws to avoid sin 227
Tip 6: Keeping demons out of your home 229
Tip 7: Removing legal ground from Satan 231
Tip 8: Principle of returning a favor 234
Tip 9: Defeating the mind-jammer spirit 236
Tip 10: Ignoring verbal entrapment 238
Tip 11: Defeating demonic setups 242
Tip 12: Demonic resistance to medication 244
Tip 13: Exercising the mind of Christ 247
Tip 14: Preventing drowsiness 249
Tip 15: Mood changers 253
Tip 16: Defeating enemy tactics 256
Tip 17: Repent of long-standing lies 258
Tip 18: Make restitution now 260
Tip 19: The role of music in deliverance 263
Tip 20: The power of the Lord's prayer 265

WARFARE DECREE **267**
Decree for house and family 268
It is further decreed: 269
Decree for our nation 271

INTERVIEW QUESTIONS AND ANSWERS **273**
RECOMMENDED DELIVERANCE RESOURCES . **281**

DEDICATED

TO THE

LIFE, LEGACY, BEAUTY, AND LOYALTY OF

NANCY E. KEKLIKIAN

FAITHFUL WIFE, MOTHER, GRANDMOTHER
ESCORTED INTO PARADISE JANUARY 22, 2016

DAVID KEKLIKIAN

ACKNOWLEDGMENTS

It is my privilege to pay tribute and thank the many who became a special part of my book-writing years. Few are well-known; most are commoners like us. Vivid testimonies reveal the outlandish truth in this hair-raising manuscript in which readers will identify some of their own problematic anomalies.

Other folks have been a strength to mind, body, and soul while this book trilogy is being wrestled to its near completion. Owing to its oppositional subject matter this volume has been battle-heavy for three years, with hard-to-describe oppositions.

My personal family of righteous heritage has mentored and prayed the Lord would develop me in the spiritual arts of loving, forgiving, receiving, and tenacity to complete a difficult documentary, for which I was not qualified, nor could be without divine help. Also, their technical skills helped to defeat frustrations due to my slow comprehension of both electronic and the ever-encroaching, devilish "phantom" technologies that ominously alter and splice human with animal genes to create freak beings.

Direct help was given by my son, John David, daughter, Deana Spyres, and her son Riley Alexander. Grandson Jackson Spyres – a professional plumber; and granddaughter Gigi Spyres, remain an inspiration through their love and manifest gifts in theater and music. Bright and beautiful toddler grandsons Milo Evan and his brother Charlie Nova Keklikian, extend our Armenian family brotherhood into another generation.

Eighty-four years of blessed memories remain vivid of my godly brother, Philip Mark Keklikian (1937-2021) who labored four decades with us in the gospel. He passed into heaven yesterday, the same day the edits of this manuscript were completed.

Clearly the Lord had ordained continuity of Philip's "Gift of Helps" [1 Corinthians 12:28], spiritual rank, talents, and anointed heritage of four generations of Armenian ministers and martyrs. These spiritual features and virtues are now conferred upon our willing, able, and obedient nephew, Mark Daniel Keklikian, and wife Micki, to close the death gap, as when the Lord prepared Joshua to succeed Moses in destroying the Lord's enemies.

Altogether, this small army has advanced my character towards that demanded of disciples.

The result is this documentary literature being read by millions. It thus fulfills more of the highly consequential prophecy the Lord forcefully pronounced over me on March 13, 1965 through apostolic evangelist Raymond H. Bloomfield, of New Zealand and Canada.

Special thanks to the staff of Village Inn Restaurants, for excellent service during this writing before, and throughout the continuing COVID-19 epidemic, which almost killed me last year at age 90. Praise be to God.

MINISTRIES AND FRIENDS
Derek Prince
Rodney G. Lensch
Paul Haglin
Virginia and George Otis, Sr.
Mary S. Becker, Prayer warrior
Peggie (Patty) Britcliffe 1936-2019
    (Subject of Deliverance Case in Book One)
Philip and Kathie Zodhiates Prison Ministry
Dr. Jim Miller, Staff, and their eloquent
    "Kindergarten Disciples", First Presbyterian
    Church, Tulsa
Others are too numerous to name.
CHRISTIAN TELEVISION PIONEERS
Pat Robertson, CBN
Lester Sumrall, World Harvest TV
Jim Bakker, PTL Network
Christian Television Network

Marcus Lamb, Daystar Network
Rejoice TV, Pensacola College

May the Lord's blessings rest upon you. Amen.

UPFRONT

Few readers will remember Evangelist Velmer Gardner who passed into eternity late in the 20th Century. My dad remembered and said of his preaching, "He was fire!" As tape recordist for the Chicago missionary conference, I saw that Dad's description was correct. The most unforgettable part this day was his extra-long altar call. A few of the 600 in attendance responded to accept Jesus Christ as their Savior. Twice he had delayed closing the service, extending the opportunity for others to make their decision. At the last, an especially holy hush came over the service as he solemnly declared, "The Lord shows me there are seventeen more of you for whom this is your last call from God before you enter eternity...you know who you are. I will wait just another moment". Over the next two minutes nine others stood and walked to the altar.

Suddenly, amid the thick silence, it struck me with horror: eight people in front of me had just been consigned to hell forever, with no more options available! It took my breath away to realize this was their Judgment Day. Several scriptures flashed into my mind: "I ceased not to warn everyone night and day..." (Acts 20:29). "Fear him...which hath power to cast into hell" (Luke 12:5). "God is not mocked" (Galatians 6:7).

Indelibly marked by that event, I renewed my dedication to warn others. Since that day, multiplied millions have died and passed into eternity - most to utter ruin. Please be impressed that for some readers today's invitation to accept Jesus' pardon will be your final opportunity. Death often comes suddenly without warning, as you know by reading obituaries. If you make the right decision now, two great blessings will overtake you:

1. Your future will be amazingly wonderful in heaven forever.

2. You will be spiritually enabled to comprehend the revelation in these pages and live free of demonic torments.

How do you do that? Believe on the Lord Jesus Christ and thou shalt be saved and thy household" (Acts 16:30-31). See also Romans 10:9-13. My prayer is that you will have made the right decision about life's singularly most critical matter. It does seem improbable and illogical that the majority of the world's population at life's end shall have ignored this gospel truth. And while the Lord has always known this, He yet has commanded believers to preach the gospel to all nations of the world. What you are reading here is one small effort to help bring it to pass.

It should be emphasized that the invisible parts of human life are the most vital for time and eternity. For example, consider mind, will, intellect, conscience, thoughts, morality, emotion, spirit, soul, and faith. Though devoid of visible properties, these are nonetheless real spiritual substance. They are not nothing. Even a child knows that when these qualities depart from grandma, her body may look the same as before, but suddenly she is unable to smile, see, speak, make decisions, or give a hug. She did not cease to exist. But the life of this sweet lady now resides somewhere else: and as her body is lowered in burial her loved ones will be exercising all those invisible qualities - shedding visible tears of invisible sadness. We must learn that God is not obligated to invite anyone a second time to accept His offer of rescue. Indeed, if He should beckon you, it would be desperately presumptuous to ignore Him because the first call might well be the last and only that is extended.

If you have not already done so, I implore you to pray these words sincerely: God be merciful to me, a sinner. Save my soul in Jesus' name. I receive Jesus now as my Savior and Lord.

DAVID KEKLIKIAN

PREFACE

Here we draw upon two points made in Derek Prince's book, War in Heaven.

Page 24: "Once a war has begun, fighting the opposition is not optional. Every citizen of a government that declares war is personally at war also." Thus, when Lucifer declared war against God in heaven, his heavenly followers - and by extension his enslaved citizens of earth, were likewise engaged. For this reason, our Lord of Armies fights the opposing forces in the heavens and on earth.

Page 28: There are more than a hundred passages of Scripture where Jehovah is called "Lord of Hosts" or "God of Hosts"; host being Old English for armies. The battles being fought are both physical and spiritual.

In military battles among nations, their respective warriors engage each other with lethal force amid the smoke, confusion, and carnage. Warfare has never been different, whether physical or spiritual. This rule applies equally in our thoughts and imaginations. Christians believe by faith that their leaders are leading them in a worthy cause, and that God is guiding their steps aright. "Lean not to thine own understanding, trust ...and He shall direct thy paths" (Proverbs 3:5). Even the strongest among us, however, do not survive to fight strenuous battles more than a hundred years. Jesus died in battle at age 33.

Following the precedent of Book One, here are eleven more detailed accounts of spiritual warfare that resulted in Christians and Jews being delivered from demons. Also, briefly shown in a chart are 25 other typical deliverances from demons. In addition, there are 20 proven tips and techniques that help us live our lives free of demonic torments. Chapters four and five provide the biblical perspective on thoughts, imaginations, voices, and on the conduct of demons, humans, and God in battle. The popular Warfare Decree in Book One is reprinted here for your personal declaration.

This substantial slice of truth is compelling, even if alarming. While it may seem narrow to some, it is all the more important because too few teachers properly report on it. Detailed spiritual clashes as reported may be jarring because their content plows deep into the soul fabric of us all. Readers of Book One have said the following:

"It's scary. I know it's true, but I can hardly believe it." "It reads like science fiction."

"I didn't know it was based on a true story – until Patty's picture reminded me of singer Patsy Cline."

"I can't read it; I'm scared."

"I couldn't finish it; it brings up too much of my past – things I was taught as a teenager in church that bothered me."

A famous medical doctor who also teaches a Sunday School class said, "I haven't finished reading your book. That's harrowing stuff. But, of course, the Bible tells us that Lucifer was an angel. So why doubt the obvious?"

Our idea is to highlight specific scriptures that have been largely ignored or spuriously kept from public discourse. They "…prove what is that good and acceptable, and perfect, will of God" (Romans 12:2). How ever imperfect my words might seem, perhaps their biblical documentation will be enough to generate honest examination of biblical deliverance by and for ordinary Christians. May you be sufficiently encouraged to heed the Lord's decrees and warnings, "…exhorting one another; and so much the more, as ye see the day approaching" (Hebrews 10:25).

God's will for disciples is to make use of both old and new technology in proclaiming the gospel. Since dark angels understand and exploit all the technological means to deceive us, Christians must likewise engage it to counter the negative.

Without definitive teaching, multitudes still question whether there is a hell. Its unfortunate inhabitants, however, are tragically certain of it. The sure answer is found in Luke 16:19-31. These thirteen verses taught by Jesus warn that we must, at all cost, seek and pray to escape such a judgment. The salient fact is expressed in Verse 24:

The rich man in hell "cried and said, Father Abraham, have mercy on me, and send Lazarus [the former beggar now in Paradise], that he may dip the tip of his finger in water, and cool my tongue; for I am tormented in this flame". Verse 28 further affirms that hell is the final "place of torment".

The mercy of receiving a single drop of water was not granted to that rich man. Over the past 2,000 years since his heart-rending appeal, he remains in the flames of hell still begging for one drop of water. That torment shall continue forever.

Through title, text, Scripture, and examples, this book displays verbally graphic pictures of the war in which each of us fight. It rages in the heavens, on earth, and in our personalities. Its obvious consequences are terrible and in evidence everywhere. But why do wars occur in the first place? They have been continuous over six thousand years. James 4:1-3 succinctly puts the question and answer this way: "From whence come wars and fightings among you? come they not hence, even of your lusts that war in your members?" Isn't it vital for us to know that? Rev. Billy Graham wrote in 1973: "I am constantly astounded that God's decrees and warnings are considered so lightly in our modern world, even among Christians" (page 108, Angels: God's Secret Agents). Jesus also warned us to "…pray always, that ye may be accounted worthy to escape all these things that shall come to pass, and to stand before the Son of man" (Luke 21:31). We must humble ourselves and pray that prayer.

That warning is more urgent now than in Jesus' day. Why? Because there remain alive more than seven billion fallen humans still in jeopardy. The real gospel of salvation is a balance of good and evil. If you are afraid to read this book, you are afraid of the Holy Bible because the facts asserted are supported by proof-scriptures in the Holy Bible. Are you brave enough and wise enough and to both read and heed them? I pray that you are.

DAVID KEKLIKIAN

CHAPTER ONE

SUPERIORITY OF HUMANS OVER EVIL SPIRITS

No treatment of this subject would be complete without showing the similarities and differences between humans and evil spirits. The most obvious difference is that humans have a physical body, while spirits do not. The first three chapters of the book of Genesis answer most of these questions.

My former teacher, Ray Bloomfield, of New Zealand, described man this way: "Man is a soul, has a spirit, and lives in a body." That made it easy for me to remember. Thus, we brilliantly conceived, three-dimensional humans are superior in every way to one-dimensional, soulish demons. It is curious that evil spirits and angels alike express many of the same traits that humans have; odd because there is no record of the time or process by which they were created, such as the record given for humans. While the Holy Bible clearly describes them and their works, few people seem to think much about that and other highly consequential facts. This is why we have restated them with Bible documentation that answers provocative questions.

Consider this concept for example: If evil spirits were in any way physical you would see them coming and going among us just as you see humans interacting with each other. Though you do not see them, spirits do, indeed, move among us unseen. Partly we know of their presence by spiritually discerning them in the seriously negative behaviors of humans.

Similarly, within the same law of physics, if a human were not housed in a physical body, he likewise would be invisible because the law of visibility does not make exceptions. Still, our personality is superior to that of demonic entities, as revealed by the Lord forgiving us our sins, once we repent, while all evil spirit entities have already been judged to eternally be unsalvageable. This is the Lord's doing.

Here now is a novel mental picture to think about. Look at present reality in reverse. For example, if demons did have physical bodies and humans did not, what you would see in daily life would be every conceivable type of uncouth spirits quarreling and fighting each other, right in your favorite restaurant, booth number 13, slopping up breakfast ham and eggs and slurping long strings of spaghetti like the clownish assassins they really are. That would probably make you as mad as it now makes them under the Lord's present regime, in which He justified and loves us but not them. Such a reality would be horrifying indeed!

Realize, however, that spirits do express traits of knowledge, memory, mind, emotion, will, and sufficient intellect to speak in human languages, and openly travel in all nations of the world without buying a ticket or showing a passport. Though many of them are just plain stupid, others are very religious, some are strategists, and some are high-level rulers. In this respect they are not so different from the world's human population. As for their religious theology, James 2:19 certifies that, like genuine Christians, "the devils also believe and tremble."

[You can hear demons quarrel, scream, and argue with ministers during live deliverances recorded on CD's and MP3, for your further research and education. See RESOURCE pages for more information.]

Besides our human spirit, our body was designed to contain only one other Spirit—the Holy One. Yet, there is enough literal space in it to house thousands of evil spirits alongside the human spirit

[See Mark 5:13 and Luke 8:27-30]. Only the tainted human spirit, however, has the potential to become righteous, and that can be accomplished only by the Spirit of Jesus Christ with our ongoing cooperation. Any other spirits inside us are invaders from Satan's kingdom of evil. As long as they reside in or on a person, their mandate is to do as much damage as they can, through torments, disease and death. Jesus, on the other hand, came that we "might have life more abundantly (John 10:10)".

Demons certainly believe in Jesus Christ and reluctantly will confess that belief as we do, such as in the Apostle's Creed. In brief, its main points are:

"I believe in God Almighty and in Jesus Christ, his Son, who was conceived of the Holy Spirit, born of a virgin, died for our sins, was buried, resurrected, and ascended to his Father in heaven, where he will judge the living and the dead."

No self-respecting demon can deny this obvious truth. They know the scriptures and have felt the agony of defeat through the power of the Word of God and the Holy Spirit. When pressed to acknowledge it, they do so. Thus, their belief, faith, and testimony are fully as orthodox as that of a Presbyterian Christian. Not widely recognized is that they attend church regularly, although their purpose is different from ours. They shudder and tremble at the anointed proclamation of the scriptures (See James 2:19). They are fully aware they have not been called to salvation but to damnation. Anointed church services may not be comfortable for them, but they have to follow orders of their commander to attend, observe, and report their findings.

Jesus cast out a legion of demons (a minimum of 2000) from the Demoniac of Gadara, all within a moment after brief conversation with them (See Mark 5:9 and Luke 8:30). That occasion is not to be regarded as a rare anomaly. As believers, we, too, are entitled, authorized, and ordered to do likewise (See Mark 16:17). In one case—exceptional due to the large number—it was my privilege to help a lady evict 600 demons, albeit not in one session. Her deliverance is detailed in the "Snarling Dog" Case in Chapter Two. She prospered and lived well twenty-six years after the demons altogether lost their position of influence. This illustrates the superiority of ordinary, non-professional believers, over evil spirits.

How remarkably complex and resilient is the human body, able to replicate barely discernable nuances of, not only our own, but also of any "unauthorized" personalities hidden within. Subtle movement in facial expressions mirror the slightest change of feelings in soul or spirit. Lifting an eyebrow is enough to cause the spirit of a lady's suitor to soar. There is the indescribable beauty of giggling little girls bubbling in joyful play, totally oblivious to their surroundings, or boisterous boys flipping marbles to gain a winning advantage. An aged grandfather may sweetly ask his young granddaughter, "How old are you?" She holds up three chubby fingers and says, "phree!" His heart melts in satisfaction, seen in his smile. Such blissful exchanges express the highest level of joyous love not afforded to angels, demons or other creatures. It is humans who are the offspring and true family of God (See Ephesians 3:14-15). God is love—its expression being far more than physical.

God sent his Son to earth, not to become an angel or spirit, that those entities who sinned might be redeemed from damnation. "...He took not on him the nature of angels; but he took on him the seed of Abraham [man]" (Hebrews 2:16). Neither angels nor demons can be conformed to the image of the Son of God. That is the exclusive privilege reserved to humans. Angels and demons have no way to mate with a counterpart and reproduce after their own kind. For this we can be thankful! They do not have the privilege of training up offspring in the way of godliness; were not "fearfully and wonderfully made" as are we (See Psalm 139:14-16). The Lord never provides help to demons or rebellious angels in desperate need of comfort. Quite to the contrary, they are without privilege and are forever damned to separation from God.

The human body is so magnificent in detail and abilities that some angels and all demons desire to live in one. Many angels so craved it that lust drove them to forsake their purely angelic first estate. Seeing how fair the daughters of men were, they used their supernatural ability to take on a physical body and sexually mate with human women. That act sealed their doom, along with the population who thus engaged the angels to reproduce freaks and giants. For this rebellion, God, in anger and grief, altogether destroyed that freakish worldwide culture in his Noahic flood (See Genesis 6:2-7). Some writers draw other conclusions from this Scripture passage, as if it were lore.

Even while demons stealthily utilize invisibility to their advantage in spiritual warfare — each having had thousands of years' experience in destroying people — demons still are no match for just one born-again believer. We have unlimited back-up and support from heaven! "When the enemy shall come in like a flood, the Spirit of the Lord shall lift up a standard against him" (Isaiah 59:19). We are the elect of God; they are the damned. Praise Him!

They can never adjust or overcome their evil nature or otherwise be transformed but are permanently stuck in evil deeds and character; are not invited to repent or to claim any blessed promise of God; can never be healed or otherwise made to feel good through any form of salvation; cannot be relieved of pain and anguish. They have no way out! There can never be a good day or better outcome for them; no free will, no choices. They are slaves of Satan, ever in misery during earth time, then finally to be sealed in hell's eternal horror chambers.

Is it any wonder that God, who exhausted the crowning riches of heaven to redeem man, shall likewise cast into hell all who prefer to indulge in demon-like behavior? God will not be ignored or scorned and is never to be mocked! (See Galatians 6:7).

The most effective military tactic is to become invisible to an enemy through technology of stealth drones, bombers, camouflage, and other mechanisms of war. Demons inherently have this tactical advantage over human adversaries. They are as literal and tormenting as they are invisible.

Motivated primarily by sensory and visible aspects of life, people are largely oblivious to invisible agents who affect our daily lives. You have heard it said, "Nothing is as it appears". That has never been more true than today, considering television, hand-held devices in the billions, motion pictures, and adjacent media through the Internet. The masses of humanity have become so enamored with bizarre and ever-flipping "holograms" that they are hardly able to concentrate on one object or subject, especially as relates to angels and demons. Thus, the evil ones have significant advantage in spiritual warfare, which is that most people do not want to believe in or seriously engage such invisible living beings as so undeniably described and encountered in the Holy Bible. I agree with the late Jesse Penn Lewis, who, in 1912, wrote in War on the Saints, "Our Creator never gave us a faculty to be misused or unused."

The superiority of humans over evil spirits is seen in every aspect of our triune construction and capability—spirit, soul, and body with added spiritual gifts, that are to be exercised with all our might to the glory of God (see Deuteronomy 6:5).

Dissipation of human faculties are futile exercises. "Love not the world, neither the things that are in the world. If any man love the world, the love of the Father is not in him" (John 2:15-16). Loving the world is unlawful love. Thus, when faculties of mind and body are unused toward God they are misused for the kingdom of Satan.

Willful failure in this regard provides ample ground for evil spirits to invade us legally. They engage us through delusion and pretense. How easy man has made it for them through today's kaleidoscopic, ever-flashing media images that are mere photographs – a deceptive and bogus substitute for biblical reality.

Except for pure teaching or documentaries, the entire image industry is pretense. While presentations of value do exist, they are few indeed. The Bible refers to "cunningly devised fables" (See

2 Peter 1:16 and 2 Timothy 4:4). This includes presentations of many religious zealots. We must learn to discern the false from the genuine.

AUDIO-VISUAL DECEPTIONS

Deceptions are proliferated through audio-visual media. Actors and actresses go to school to learn the art of pretending. They substitute their true name for a false one - a stage name, that creates a false personality—or public image. From that time forward they pretend. Their true selves are set aside. Rarely does an actor let the public see or know much about their personal lives. Acting out the false image in public appearances deepens the deception. Ominously, this is exactly the kind of work that demons do, pushing aside one's true personality and displacing it with their own.

Generally, it is fictional stories that are born in a writer's imagination and produced as a film or stage play. It will be performed by the actor's artificial personality. This requires another layer of pretense.

The new role demands its own false name because the previous one does not fit the new fiction. This latter is now called "my character", which lasts until another is taken on. Here we have the original false personality overlaid by another to enact the script that emanated from someone else's imagination. It usually involves foolishness, brutality, or immorality, and is always laced with conflict. Did you notice the spirits involved in this scenario? Foolishness, Brutality, Immorality, and Conflict are the names and specialties of demonic spirits.

In a further pretense, the actor now must stir his own imagination, draw from "within himself", and personally interpret the caricature of the other guy's imaginary character. His hope is that a supreme performance will find favor for an Academy Award. To achieve it, he must memorize words that were written by somebody else, while pretending to be the imaginary character, convincingly speak the lines with a feigned accent appropriate to the scene. The foolishness does not end there. For the very manner in which he speaks must be directed by a director's interpretation and made to match the movements, emotions, and speaking style of the character, thus further distancing his true self from reality, stressing over the conflicting points of view among the two or more pretenders. Again, it does not end there! Do not overlook the cameraman, costume and set designers; stunt men, prop man, make-up artists, and the other hundred helpers, attendants, and countless extras paid to help authenticate the farce. Finally, there is the shooting location. Australia is now simulated in New Mexico; Western mountains are now in Italy; and the Congo is swampland Florida. The ship Titanic is a model boat in a tank of water agitated by a group of paid paddlers, using trick photography to make the deception more believable. Nothing is done in real time, for an entire panorama of decades must be completed for viewing within in a 90-minute to 3-hour time frame.

After decades of adapting to myriad personalities that conclude one's pretense career, one's original soul is left to wonder who he really is. One famous actor was quoted near the time of his death, asking in bewilderment, "Is this all there is?" He died at age 49, having ignored the one Personality, he should have emulated — that of Jesus Christ.

Demons of false personality are adept at seizing opportunities to infiltrate. Many actors become alcoholic, drug addicted, delusional, die an early death, or commit suicide. Most are divorced from multiple spouses—some as many as eight times, between other engagements with concubines and facelift surgeons. Will this charade ever cease? No.

Ardent viewers of such pretenses also are unavoidably affected in their own outlook toward reality. Many will model one or more of their favorite characters, mimicking them for inclusion into their own personality. Who hasn't heard or seen a guy doing his imitation of, say, "Hey, watch me do Jimmy Cagney!" Or Elvis, or someone else. Mimicking of a violent character is worse. Thus, delusion is propagated at every level, including the mind of the viewer. Fictions are undergirded by demons of pretense, false personality, delusion, and a host of others. They are the source - the door openers. Within this systematic framework, actors often open their lives to invasion by malevolent spirits who deeply immerse themselves into the personalities of their various "characters", such as drunkard, drug addict, murderer, rapist, playboy, harlot, gunslinger, Santa Claus, homosexual, tough guy, etc. No self-respecting demon would pass up such opportunities to enter into and "help" the actor reach the pinnacle of his role. Doing so is what earns him an Academy Award among like-minded peers — reproducing after their own kind.

These facts apply not only to professional, intentional actors, but bleed into the antics, exaggerations, hypocrisies, or delusions found in Christian believers who fall from grace, whether in pulpit or pew. The Holy Bible is full of warnings, admonitions, and examples that reveal the follies of our sin nature.

The ruse that "seeing is believing" has become such a staple in our vocabulary that to believe in the invisible realm is often considered to be a symptom of insanity. Yet, our health of mind and body depends upon believing and reacting to what generally cannot be seen. We know that the use of powerful electron microscopes is required to reveal tiny particles or life forms, to the end that what is really there might become visible to researchers. What applies in the literal microcosm applies even more to the truly invisible. Such obvious intangibles as spirit, faith, hope, mind, will, intellect, emotion, conscience, memory, air—in constant use by everyone—cannot be made visible by any earthly means. In man's effort to make the invisible become visible, physical idols are crafted of wood, mud, hay, and stubble. Multitudes dedicate their lives in tortuous worship of this lifeless garbage. Even so, demons oblige by attaching to the idols, to grow stronger through receiving worship. In view of all of this, it should not be a stretch for you to accept the realities of our subject that are so well documented.

No doubt you have read reports of those whose lives have been transformed for the better by embracing facts revealed in the Holy Bible. My purpose is to present pertinent facts with such convincing evidence that you may clearly understand this little-discussed dimension of good and evil in your life. Once understood, you may apply effective solutions to problems which heretofore have escaped scientific, medical, psychological, or religious diagnoses and effective treatments. That is what it did for me. What a joy it is to be free of ominous, foreboding torments, fears and pains, long believed to be inescapable. May you become sufficiently daring to take this new step in faith. Let this be your personal springboard to freedom. Desperate people will readily seek for help. Why wait? The Lord will help anyone who is determined to find truth.

DEMONS RELEASE BODY PARTS

There is no part of the human anatomy or personality in which a demon has not resided or tormented. It is instructive to know their work is specific to certain body parts, where symptoms usually can be analyzed. One demon does not occupy the entire body. In rare instances, however, a victim may become a total demoniac driven by multiple demons.

These twenty-five human parts shown below were individually host to demons. Also shown are several types of their destructive work, and cities where I was privileged to cast them out. While far from complete, the list is representative enough to make the point. Demons use our bodies as a residence, much like "hotel rooms". Until discovered, they are free to enter and depart their residence at will. Our purpose is to apprise unwitting victims of their tactics and presence, so as to mount effective countermeasures. Without this knowledge, they cannot be defeated, nor their negative effects healed. Whatever part of your body that historically has given you the most trouble or pain should be given the most precautionary care and maintenance.

You may have used some of the following words in ordinary conversation at some time: fingerhold, toehold, foothold, stronghold. Whatever the context of their general use, these words also describe the progression of bondage a demon typically secures. A fingerhold would be the least debilitating, as well as being the most readily accessible to a demon such as in cigarette smoking, drinking of alcohol, etc. Once fastened, he would move from that secured position to the next sequential levels – a toehold, foothold, and finally a stronghold. This gives you an idea of their stealthy progression in bringing one into ever greater bondage. Consider this principle as you study the chart,

LOCATION	PERSONS	BODY PARTS	AFFLICTIONS
Hollywood, St. Louis, Kansas	2 Men 1 Woman	Fingers	Arthritis
St. Louis	1 Man 2 Women	Legs	Muscle Cramp Spasms
St. Louis	2 Women	Bowels	Backed up 4 weeks and 2 months
Los Angeles	Woman	Brain Tumor	Cause: Scientology Dianetics
St. Louis	Man	Brain Tumor	Died after 6 months remission
St. Louis	Woman	Brain Tumor	Healed, but re-curred ultimately
Chicago	Man	Eyes	Lust
Chicago	Woman	Eyes	Blindness
St. Louis	Man	Ears	Ringing, brief deafness
Fenton, MO	Man	Head	Crippling Migraine
St. Louis & Tulsa	2 Women	Head	Migraine

LIBERATION OF MIND, WILL, AND INTELLECT

LOCATION	PERSONS	BODY PARTS	AFFLICTIONS
Camp in Georgia	Myself	Private Parts	Demon named "Big Dick" expelled
Chicago	Several Male & Female	Private Parts	Masturbation, itch, fungus, homosexual, stench
S. Bend, IN/St. Louis, MO	4 Women	Womb	Barren, One after 8 abortions
Illinois	Woman	Womb	Barren - later bore children
Festus, MO	Man	Short Leg	Leg instantly grew 1 ½ inches
Los Angeles/Tulsa, OK	Myself	Nose	Years of severe itch
Camp in Georgia	Man	Nose	Spirit of sinus expelled
Los Angeles, CA	Myself	Kidney	Stone departed with spirit
St. Louis	2 Women	Breasts	Miniature in mother & daughter; normalized
St. Louis & Los Angeles	2 Men	Teeth	Cavities supernaturally filled with gold and porcelain fillings
St. Louis	My Dad	Blood	Healed of Leukemia
Various	Men & Women	Chronic Disease	Instantly corrected
Lo Angeles	1 Woman	Back	Severe Spasm
Los Angeles	Myself	Low Back	Demon shown in x-ray - expelled
Chicago	1 Man	Sciatica, Scoliosis	Corrected

33

LOCATION	PERSONS	BODY PARTS	AFFLICTIONS
St. Louis	My Brother	Heart infirmity	Aneurism, murmur (heart healed, died 5 years later of cancer)
Omaha, NE	Woman	Lungs	Asthma-cured
Tulsa, OK	Woman	Stomach	Bloated by spirit of false pregnancy, Cured.
Ventura, CA	Mother & Daughter	Gluttony	Simultaneously cured
St. Louis	Man	Crooked Face	Straightened
St. Louis	Woman	Face	Demon transmuted face to snarling dog baring fangs, then restored to normal
Tulsa	Man	Allergies	Debilitation stopped
Tulsa	2 Women	Arm could not be raised	Instantly released
Tulsa	Woman	Voices	Terrible torment. Stopped.

Two facts may be observed in relation to the above listing.

1. Most of these miracles resulted when only this author and the candidate acted together with the Lord, on the basis of Acts 1:8: "But ye shall receive power after that the Holy Ghost [Spirit] is come upon you." Combine that with Luke 10:19: "Behold, I give unto you power to tread on (types of demons called) serpents and scorpions,

and over all the power of the enemy, and nothing shall by any means hurt you."

2. In deference to Matthew 10:8, no money or merchandise was mentioned or received:

"Heal the sick, cleanse the lepers, raise the dead, cast out devils [demons]; freely ye have received, freely give" (Matthew 10:8 – also see Mark 16:15-18).

It is also a fact that not every part of a human dies at the same time. In most cases, by the time one reaches the age of 90, for example, parts of the body and mind have become dysfunctional in part or altogether. Certain parts likely will have been removed by surgery to prevent "a rotten apple from destroying the whole barrel". Functions of the mind, will, and intellect likewise will have been altered, as well as one's physical appearance. Much or most of the debilitation will have been induced by the stress of battling demons, even if denied by medics and theologians. Keeping feeble and limping old people alive is one of the biggest businesses on earth, which is testimony to the above facts. Every kind of sickness and disease is a branch of death, which left unchallenged, will often hasten one's death and burial.

Realize that ordinary true Christians can perform extraordinary feats in person, anywhere, any time. No crowd of people is necessary. No salaried "professionals" need be present. No denomination of religion need sponsor or approve of it, and no money need be requested or exchanged for God's miraculous blessings to flow. No one will get rich by doing in the same way what Jesus did and commanded be done by his followers. "...a rich man shall hardly enter into the kingdom of heaven" (Matthew 19:23-24). The just shall live by faith (Romans 1:17)...moreso when uncompromised by money.

The original gospel of Jesus Christ resides within every true believer, "...for behold the kingdom of God is within you" (Luke 17:21). Again, Matthew 12:28: "If I cast out devils by the Spirit of God, then the Kingdom of God has come unto you." It is to be manifested – seen, heard, demonstrated – by each one of us in fellowship. Ephesians 4:11-12 "...perfecting of [all] the saints for the work of the ministry." That Kingdom of God within you has neither constraints nor restrictions and is to be demonstrated and seen wherever you may live and go. I hasten to add, however, that more than two or three believers praying together is entirely proper for engaging in this type of ministry, though others are not needed in most cases.

WHAT CAN BELIEVERS DO?

Suppose that every Christian believer were taught the Scriptures and shown how to put them into practice in accordance with Jesus' teaching.

These are disciples. Suppose further that only 25% of devout believers (maybe 200 million) were to act out the gospel once a year for five years. Many might be described as were apostles Peter and John: "unlearned and ignorant men" (Acts 4:13). However, if only those few performed acts similar to those shown in the chart above, consider the impact it would make having three billion demons neutralized. Believers who were thus cured could also reproduce such feats for an even wider effect. That would be catastrophic for Satan, who has no replacements!

The scriptures and testimonies that comprise Chapter Two illustrate every believer's superiority and authority over demons and emphasize the nature of the warfare that Christians inevitably face.

No single demon can overpower a knowledgeable believer, and no demon has ever cast out a human spirit. However, one may attach to a single part of the body and attempt to establish a base of operation. If successful and not recognized, that base will be expanded and become further populated with kindred spirits.

What is true of the body is also true of the soul — i.e., mind and emotions. These may likewise become warped or impaired by demonic intrusion. Apart from applying the word and power of God, demons inside a person cannot be defeated and removed.

If we would adopt the policy of "each one, teach one", then we could come together "on the first day of the week", and each one of us publicly testify of "the wondrous works of the Lord" (Acts 20:7).

What follows should be reassuring to Christians in general, but prickly to skeptics. This array of believers' deliverances reveals the commonality of human need everywhere. A victim's persona, background, age, social standing, religion, or mental acuity has no bearing upon demonic torments. Satan is not a "respecter of persons". His deceptions that cause misery, pain, persecution, bondage, and murders, are indiscriminate. Everyone is a target.

Among the fifteen cases detailed in books one and two are Presbyterians, Catholics, Pentecostals, Lutherans, Baptists, Jews, Scientologists, and several unlabeled. Their employments variously ranged from chiropractor, machinist, choir singers, church deacons, ordained ministers, foreign missionaries, university president, mortgage banker, waitress, college student, registered nurse, business executive, and more. Their various bondages and afflictions were not unusual, but typical. Keep this variety in mind as you read the following eleven reports. Realize that you can lay hands on not only others, but also on yourself, and command an offending spirit to depart from you. Mimic what I have done and explained in these cases and give commands in the same way. Every true believer in Jesus Christ has been given authority to do so (Luke 10:19), though two in agreement are better than one alone. However, if you have done wrong, it must be acknowledged and repented of beforehand, in order to remove any legal standing a demon may have gained. Do not miss this opportunity to free yourself from bondage. If you do not do this for yourself, who will? Probably less than ten percent of professional ministers even acknowledge the various works of demons against Christians, let alone deal with them.

The following paragraph is borrowed from the foreword I wrote for The Awesome Power of Your Faith, published in 1978 by Ray Bloomfield:

> *Thoughts and imaginations are on the inside. Feelings and emotions are on the inside. Spiritual gifts are received on the inside. Spiritual battles are fought from the inside. Physical healings work from the inside. Personal deliverance from demon bondage is exerted from the inside. "The Kingdom of God is within you" (Luke 17:21).*

If the Kingdom of God were the only one within you, life would be as perfect as Paradise. But that is not the case. Satan's kingdom is there also. In the clearest terms and examples the details of the deliverances that follow reveal the little understood source of our most vexing pains and miseries and show the way to end them. These 11 cases illustrate that no one is unaffected by satanic forces. Hundreds of powerless religions offer zero protection and, in fact, are Satan's snare of choice, because nearly everyone is religious. Moderate Christianity is of some help, but in diluted form is deceptive delusion. Ephesians six shows that a Christian's protection is his proactive use of defensive and offensive weapons designed to defeat spiritual enemies. Without vibrant belief and use of the armor he is little better off than a non-believer in regard to protection.

Moreover, believers have carried with them their lawless history and inheritance up to the moment of repentance. The "old nature" and its spiritual baggage, previously hidden by ignorance, becomes more energized and animated in conflict with the newly shared residency of the Holy Spirit. That condition prevails until one's death, with both "sides" suffering casualties.

The four gospels of the New Testament present the warfare that Jesus fought and taught. The Acts, letters, and books of the apostles present the do's, don'ts and warnings of how to fight and win. The following reports demonstrate these facts, some of which undoubtedly characterize your personal life battles.

CHAPTER TWO

DETAILED CASES OF EXORCISM

DEMONS GANG-RAPE A LADY

There had been many helps to this lady in house maintenance, lawn mowing, repair of dangerous concrete porch steps, multiple auto repairs, and more, plus cash gifts. One afternoon at her home, she blurted out, "Why are you doing this? Do you love me?! That stunning question had never been put to me by others I had helped. I didn't have a ready answer. Three times she repeated with increasing urgency, "Why are you doing this? Do you love me? Do you love me!?"

It was clear that she did not understand why I wanted to help, and she needed an answer. No one else had helped in her desperation. I hesitated to answer, for if I were to answer "Yes," she might erroneously think there would be relief coming via a budding romance, only to suffer another hurt. That would have compounded her problem. If I replied, "No," she might have misunderstood, which would add to the rejection and shame already overwhelming her. After a moment of mentally asking the Lord, wisdom came. I replied, "Jesus loves you". Whereupon she burst into tears and cried openly.

Gaunt, tall, and exceedingly thin, her disposition was pleasant, friendly, and she was efficient in her waitress work. Having served me often, this day she was especially downcast and seemed compelled to confidentially confess her problem amid tears, hanging her head in shame. Over an extended period of time, she was being forcibly gang-raped by demons, multiple times every single night. She was exhausted from both the lack of sleep and the ongoing horror of uncontrollable rapes. That miserable circumstance was the cause of her emaciated physical condition and wretched shame, all kept secret for fear of scorn and mockery. The worst pangs of hellish torments are generally kept private until they become intolerable.

She explained that her husband had killed himself by gunshot to the head, right in front of her and their small son, which ended their turbulent marriage. Depression drove her to alcoholic drunkenness.

She now lived in a small house, rented from her employer.

In her usual half-drunken state, I asked her to sit down. Seeing her quivering in deep agony of soul, crying tears of hopelessness, her bony knees knocking together and teeth chattering, my heart was smitten with anguish and compassion – ever remembering like miseries in my lonely youth, having no one to help, understand, or confide in. Today as I tell this story, I weep at the memory of her. I also remember that Jesus wept when moved with compassion upon seeing such kinds of hell on earth (See John 11:35 and Mark 9:22).

My spirit angrily burst forth in a language of the Holy Spirit as the Lord assaulted the demon invaders, pushing them back from the forefront of her personality. Within moments, she began to recover her senses. I briefly explained the gospel that would save her, and that together we would command the tormentors to depart from her body and soul. She nodded her head to acknowledge her understanding and agreed in hope of help. I led her in a prayer, confessing her sins, turning away from them, and asking Jesus to forgive her and live His life in her from this time forward.

In anger, I demanded, "You foul spirits of horror, rape, lust, torment, terror, shame, fear, bondage, drunkenness, and poverty! Pay attention to the Word of the Lord! You have lost this house! You no longer have any right to live here! Set yourselves in order. Now, GET OUT OF THIS HOUSE! In Jesus' mighty name, you are unable to resist the word of the Lord, the anointing of the Holy Spirit, and the Blood of Jesus Christ. You are defeated and vanquished. Depart in Jesus' mighty name! Cease and desist. Expire and come out of her!"

Forced to hear and acknowledge the truth, and cowering from the assault, they no longer had a choice. She began to expel forcefully and out they came, one after another, through retching coughs and regurgitation. Soon she was relieved of her oppressors and began to smile weakly in awe of the wondrous thing that had happened. "Now Cheryl," I directed, "Ask the Holy Spirit to come in and fill all the rooms of your soul that have just been vacated." She eagerly obeyed, lifted her arms heavenward, took in a deep breath, and widened her smile with renewed strength.

Success having been achieved, I blessed her in prayer and turned to depart, knowing the next time she served my table it would be with a happy smile instead of a shamed face. And that is exactly how it unfolded over the ensuing weeks that I remained in her city.

Demons were cast out and her life was redeemed and preserved. Colleagues at the restaurant quickly noticed her change of demeanor and optimistic outlook. Her new life was off to a good start. To be expected after years of continuous struggle, the enemy would counterattack from time to time. Life was certainly better, but not always easy. This is the usual way life proceeds after a major deliverance from a long-standing oppression.

Compassion needs corresponding action to be of any practical use. May we ever heed the Lord's prompting of genuine compassion for bewildered victims who live among us. They are not "irregulars", as some describe them, but potentially sons and daughters of God. Christians are instructed to become weaponized warriors and take the initiative in opposing the works and workers of the devil. Our presence should be such that it causes "the devils to believe and tremble" (James 2:19).

This deliverance is a clear example of trauma opening the door to demonic invasion. If you question whether a demon could actually rape someone, consider how they physically tormented numerous victims whom Jesus healed by casting out demons. Once inside, they are able to torment any part of the human body or soul. Rape is no exception.

STACY AND THE ROARING LION

President of Trinity Bible College, Dr. Charles Duncombe, said, "David, I think I have some ministry for you.", then introduced me to Stacy, a male student from Italy. Over the previous two years

Stacy could sleep only ten minutes at a time several times a night. Exhaustion rendered him barely functional. No medical cause had been found. An appointment was made for Stacy's counseling and prayer at our nearby home. I was confident in the methods, prayers, and techniques previously used in working wonders, 100% effective with no exceptions, as far as I remember. There was every reason to believe this effort would be no different.

Counseling began at midday, and continued until direct prayer at 6:00 p.m. I exercised everything I knew with fervor and integrity. Yet, after nine grueling hours there had been only meager results. Lesser spirits were expelled, but the necessary breakthrough did not happen. Major bondage remained. This had never happened before. Frustrated, I excused myself from Stacy for a moment and stepped to the far corner of the room, where I quietly appealed to the Lord: "I am absolutely exhausted. I cannot do any more. I've tried everything. I might have enough strength to try just once more – I'll give you 20 minutes, and if you don't do it by then, well, it just won't get done!" Today I can almost hear Jesus' disciples similarly asking [Mark 9:28-29]: "And when he was come into the house, his disciples asked him privately, why could not we cast him out? And he said unto them, "This kind can come forth by nothing, but by prayer and fasting." I thought my preparation had been sufficient because it was my practice to fast before praying. But there was a slight deficiency in one other department. After such a presumptuous but honest arrogance, I was to be sharply humbled. Wearily walking back to Stacy, I placed my left hand on his forehead, as before, thinking to pray and perspire through the final twenty minutes I had committed to. But instead, to my amazement, the demon instantly screwed up Stacy's face and began to roar like a lion – so loudly that it shocked me and seriously frightened our two young children in their bedrooms at the other end of the house! Both John and Deana ran out of their rooms to the hallway crying in fear of the lion roars, like they had heard at the zoo! Except, this was not the zoo. Nancy scurried over to hug them and give comfort, (and maybe explain that Daddy David was killing another lion? They knew the Bible stories. But as actor John Wayne might say, "Not hardly!). It had taken the Lord less than two seconds to answer resoundingly! Roaring several times in bluffing defiance, the spirit shook Stacy's clenched fist two inches from my face, straining to strike, but the blows were supernaturally prevented. Now broken, he manifested briefly, then flew out with a long and terrifying roar – and I mean a lion's roar! In 1 Peter 5:8-9a it is clearly revealed: "Be sober, be vigilant; because your adversary the devil, as a roaring lion, walketh about, seeking whom he may devour: Whom resist steadfast in the faith." Friend, that Scripture is more than symbolic! Do not be deceived, Satan truly roars like a lion –

and once you've experienced it, all doubt is removed forever. Another point to note is that devour does not mean a little bite, but total consumption.

Stacy fell to the floor with a thud and appeared to be as dead as a gunnysack of potatoes. He looked so dead that I wondered whether any life remained in him. I thought, "What will I do if he's really dead? That would have serious legal implications, not easy to explain. In fact, who would believe such an incredulous story? I could hardly believe it myself! I could just see me standing before the judge trying to explain this man's death only because I spoke a few words and gently laid my hands on him. Have you ever been handcuffed and helpless? Think about it ... newsmen, photographers, television reporters, flashing lights, and a barrage of questions. Reputations are ruined by lesser events.

Stunned for a half minute while evaluating, I put those questions out of my mind, slowly walked over, bent down, and softly asked, "Stacy? Can you hear me? Are you okay?" Slowly he opened his eyes, almost as a waking corpse, and weakly nodded, "Yes". Whew! That was a relief. In slow motion, I stretched out my hands to help, and with deliberate effort he slowly stood upright.

A similar event that confirms the reality of such an episode is in Mark 9:17-29, where Jesus cast a dumb spirit out of a youngster. Here is the precedent: (Verses 26-27) "And the spirit cried, and rent him sore, and came out of him: and he was as one dead; insomuch that many said, He is dead. But Jesus took him by the hand and lifted him up; and he arose." Please read that fascinating and heartrending account of a boy's father appealing to Jesus for help in verses 17 through 29.

Now standing, Stacy's face slowly opened with a grin of gratitude, almost as if in disbelief. He lifted his hands to the Lord in thanksgiving and praise, knowing he would never again be a pitiful insomniac. We rejoiced together, realizing that tonight he would enjoy a long awaited, full night of continuous sleep. I still have the smiley photograph of Stacy and me standing at our doorstep after this deliverance in midtown Tulsa, Oklahoma.

The Lord's vital lesson to me is found in John 15:5b, "...without me ye can do nothing. And in Mark 10:27 "... With men it is impossible, but not with God; for with God all things are possible". So says the Lord Jesus Christ. That lesson is forever sealed in my heart and mind. As you can see from my embarrassing effort, it is possible for a young minister on his spiritual "honeymoon" to become a little cocky with "his" tremendous successes. So much so, that after a few years it seems he could perform supernatural works by exerting more of himself and his formula, effectively dismissing the Lord from the scene. Such prideful deception creeps in through one's own evil nature. The Lord describes

Satan-the-serpent, as "... more subtle than any beast of the field ..." (Genesis 3:1). Our adamic nature is like that; ever subtly attempting to supplant the Spirit of Christ. If we fail to guard ourselves, Christ will sharply remind us of such foolishness. Thanks be to God. A question has arisen as to whether this particular roaring lion was Satan in person (1 Peter 5:8). The answer is uncertain because it cannot be proved. I was so shocked at the suddenness it did not occur to me to ask his name! There was no time for a formal introduction amid all the roaring and threatening.

However, it is curious that Satan is the only person in all of Scripture about whom the Lord has informed us: "... your adversary the devil, as a roaring lion, walketh about seeking whom he may devour." In 43 years of such ministry and acquaintances, plus a search of Old and New Testaments, there is no report of any other than the devil who roars out as a lion from inside a human.

The roaring devil limits his personal appearances to assault the few who dedicate themselves to expose and destroy his agents and the "works of the devil". On that basis it is logical that he would engage me at some point, because my purpose, declaration, and practice over decades had been to expose and destroy his works. Moreover, in this episode it absolutely required direct intervention of the Lord to dethrone him from Stacy. As stated above, I had already expended all my strength and authority in exorcising the lesser demons, before finding it impossible to dislodge the roaring lion. Fortunately, as every good parent does, God helps his children – as he did in this case. Let us be encouraged and thankful that we do not fight the devil alone, for the Spirit of Almighty God stands beside us, ready to intervene – if we will just stop long enough to ask Him! "The angels of the Lord encampeth round about them that fear him, and delivereth them" (Psalm 34:7).

LADY'S FACE MUTATES TO SNARLING DOG

Monsters portrayed in Hollywood films often are a near replica of real demons. While the fantasies appear to be exaggerated, their characteristics are no more outlandish than those described in the Bible books of Revelation and Daniel. For example, Chapter 12, verse 3 of Revelation describes "a great red dragon, having seven heads and ten horns, and seven crowns upon his heads".

Chapter 13, verse 2: "… the beast which I saw was like unto a leopard, and his feet were as the feet of a bear, and his mouth as the mouth of a lion, and the dragon gave him his power…"

The description of a beast in Daniel 7:7 gives Hollywood producers an image to build upon. Their depictions of odd, fearsome, or imaginary creatures are not surprising. Yet, in reality, sometimes a demon inhabiting a human can twist his victim largely into the shape, appearance, sound, and physical movements of an animal. I have encountered demons that caused victims to act as a slithering serpent, a roaring lion, meowing cat, and in Peggy's case, the actual transmutation of her physical countenance into a fanged, growling, attack dog - right in front of me. This is that case.

The incremental stages of a certain demon's approach, from inception in childhood, to the manifest overtaking of her as an adult, are revealed in this synopsis of Peggy's life. A "door opener" spirit entered into her and made a way for the spirit of bestiality to enter, and for other spirits to follow. It began when she was five years old. Peggy had been placed with a teenage boy relative alone in a side room. That arrangement was convenient for their parents to enjoy grownup fellowship without being interrupted by children. As ultimately reported during private counsel, the little girl was shown the private parts of her teenage cousin and encouraged to play with them as her new "toy." She later expressed amazement and childish intrigue at the phenomenon, which "seemed to come alive, to grow and release" under her control. It became the secret game they played whenever the two were placed together without supervision.

The boy's motive, of course, was to express his

hormonal lust – quite common for a teenager. However, for this naive little girl - an only child - it was a truly "fascinating game she was gleefully learning to play with him." The separate playroom isolation was oft repeated during their parents' regular gatherings. As knowledgeable ministers would suspect, an evil spirit, whose name and work are Oral Sex, entered into her, ensuring that the spirit's game would become her permanent bondage. In addition to that first spirit, there soon developed a revulsion and fear of live turtles, after seeing one slowly walking with head and neck bobbing in motions similar to that of the "toy".

The game became locked in as a way of life for her and was not limited to the boy relative. The next to be similarly engaged by her was her mid-size, male pet dog. This additional sexual relationship persisted over four years to her age of nine, all the while toying with the teenage boy as well. There was no other form of carnal desire practiced during her formative years, which remained a well - guarded secret between her and her playmate, even into adulthood.

She later became engaged to a college educated man, not revealing her long interlude of bestiality. When they were married, their sexual intimacy included what she had practiced from the age of five. It had become compulsive and the spirit behind it was deeply entrenched. In the marriage bed more conventional intimacy also was introduced. Fueled by excessive alcohol, her husband was rough, inconsiderate, and difficult to satisfy. His lust grew to engage her in sodomy. He also developed a ravenous appetite for his wife's breast milk, which accumulated when she became pregnant. In an attempt to avert this new and painful aspect of intimacy, she had her breasts professionally bound by her doctor, flat against her chest, near the time of their daughter's birth. This defensive solution, however, created a new and unexpected problem. Having been tightly bound over a long period, her breasts never returned to a normal size or shape but remained abnormally small and flat. During the unnatural breast-binding period, an evil spirit of that character found a way to enter. Long after the physical binding had ceased, the demonic entity retained control of that part of her body and kept her breasts bound in distortion. As often happens, that same spirit, prior to birth, transferred into her baby girl, so that both were to be plagued for decades with flat, undeveloped breasts.

From a deliverance standpoint, there was need on all sides. Emotional and physical damage had been done. The mother's spiritual knowledge was limited to the form and doctrine of Presbyterian services and preaching, which did not provide for exorcism. Yet, without it there could be no solution to her plight. The problem was not organic but spiritual.

At a propitious moment, I explained that invisible

entities of evil actually exist and sometimes enter into human beings. When I invited her to a house meeting where exorcism was sometimes provided, she exclaimed, "David, you are scaring me!" Though reluctant, she consented to attend. During a quiet time in a room with the pastors, the Holy Spirit soon rose up, such that I forcefully exhorted in indignation, "We don't have to put up with this!" Whereupon, I quickly stood and walked to her chair, laid my right hand on her forehead, and in Jesus' name commanded the demons of torment, guilt, and shame to get out of her body. Startled by the suddenness, the demons could put up little resistance and promptly departed from her amid manifestations of coughing and retching. In euphoric amazement, from that moment her life took a new and wonderful direction with further counseling and healings. More exorcisms occurred later. On one occasion, her breasts miraculously increased two full sizes. That occasion was the first time Peggy smiled so widely that all her teeth showed! What makes that noteworthy is that her teeth had become deformed through the excessive maluses of her mouth. Shame and embarrassment (also names of demons) had prevented her from smiling. An extension of the same miracle was that her daughter, having had the identical problem by spiritual inheritance, was likewise set free. Not only that, but her then married daughter's medically confirmed barrenness was rendered null and void when she proudly gave birth to two children, after experiencing two earlier miscarriages. Both mother and daughter were water baptized in the Meremac River as public witness of their new-found faith in Jesus Christ.

Parenthetically, on a different occasion a similar mother-to-daughter spirit transfer was witnessed in a Ventura, California meeting. While praying for the mother's deliverance, the spirit named Gluttony, was regurgitated from both at the same time. They were 30 feet from each other, and the daughter had not even known of her need! The command for the demon to depart from her mother forced the same spirit in her daughter to flee at the same time. One prayer did double duty.

Peggy's demonic bondage was extraordinary. The colony of evil spirits inside was significant enough that satanic overlords had sent an emissary once each year to observe her life and conduct. On those occasions her room would suddenly be flooded with a brilliant light. Peggy did not know what it was about, only that the event recurred annually. Because the "wonder light" did not cause anything observably negative she had said nothing about it. After multiple sessions of effective deliverance, however, the colony was sufficiently demolished that the annual wonder light visits altogether ceased. The demonic overlords had lost their colony in total defeat. Second Corinthians 11:14 explains it this way: "And no marvel; for Satan himself is transformed into an angel of light."

At best count, about 600 demons were defeated and expelled, which brought healing to her back, eliminated an incurable body stench, cured leg cramps, cleared blurry eyes, dislodged a bowel obstruction, provided a fix for her teeth, and more.

Through all the glories, there was one unforgettable deliverance moment. During a time of concentrated prayer for her, the demon beast who had entered into Peggy through sexual engagement with her childhood pet, suddenly manifested wildly through her. He literally transformed her face into the configuration of a growling, snarling dog, baring fangs in threatening defiance. The suddenness and ferocity shocked me. In near disbelief, my hair stood on end and a shiver went down my spine. Moreover, that dog was manifestly snarling right into my face! I had never seen the like of it.

Having been eight years in the Hollywood movie business and seen my share of horror films, this was like a scene in the movie "Wolfman", except that her fangs were smaller and there was no coat of fur as exaggerated in the movie. It was the highest degree of demonic manifestation I had ever witnessed—even beyond a serpent-demon hissing like a snake while Dixie's body slithered across the floor and between the chairs at the feet of my wife and me. The serpent episode occurred at Faith Tabernacle in

Chicago and likewise had been horrifyingly chilling - almost unbelievable.

As suddenly as the canine demon in Peggy manifested so ferociously, a spiritual anger rose up to energize me. I commanded, "You spirit of a dog! I command you to come out of her in Jesus' name!" It was as though we were opponents barking in a deadly dog fight ... as indeed we were! Soon, he backed down and his fearsome appearance began to recede. Then he heeled, and departed from her, in lowering growls of defeat. Peggy's appearance almost instantly transformed back into the face of the lady she really was. The Lord be praised!

Later, I asked Peggy whether she remembered the growling and barking, or the transformation of her face. She hardly remembered any of it. But to me it is unforgettable. From experience I can tell you it is fairly common for a human personality to be so totally set aside in a supernatural battle, that the victim does not fully know or remember all that had taken place. The victim's personality can temporarily be literally displaced, suppressed, or subjugated by the demon personality during a heated and bitter confrontation. That is why I have, on a few occasions, made a tape recording for the victims to later play back, as proof that my testimony to them was factual. In more recent times, ministers, such as Bob Larson and Win Worley, have made video recordings of live deliverances. Copies may still be available for purchase from their organizations, shown in the Resource pages of this book.

This event demonstrates the biblical injunction that when any two engage in sexual relations they thereby become one flesh. That union normally occurs through a proper marriage that produces human offspring, but in all unsanctioned such events it is also true of the "fleshly" souls. This principle applies whether the act is between man with woman, woman with woman, man with man, or man or woman with an animal. It also occurred when angelic "sons of God" [Genesis 6:4] mated with human women. See Genesis 3:24 and Matthew 19:5-6. The principle is further explained in 1 Corinthians 6:16. "What? Know ye not that he which is joined to a harlot is one body? For two, saith he, shall be one flesh." Outside the sanctity of the marriage covenant, ungodly soul ties are secured through sexual encounters, and the souls of the participants—no matter who, how many, or what creature they belong to - angelic, demonic, or animal—are bound together. Where multiple partners in sexual relations have taken place, the soul ties are more in number and the effects more damaging. Another principle of Scripture also applies: "... a threefold cord is not quickly broken" (Ecclesiastes 4:12b). With difficulty I broke 32 soul ties in counseling one lady, through her confession and renunciations of each and every sex partner by name. Deliverance from multiple demons followed her sincere repentance and confession. To be effective and permanent, there are no shortcuts to the scriptural process of biblical deliverance, as demonstrated by Jesus and his disciples. After extended deliverance ministry to Peggy, all aspects of her life progressively became so purified that she once happily exclaimed, "David, I really feel like a virgin now!" She was soon enabled to start her own business, make successful investments, and become a proud grandmother of several children. While her transformation took place over two years, the starting point was her willingness to explore and then acknowledge the reality of her demonic bondage, and to seek freedom. It also was important that she had a mentor-pastor whom she could trust to keep confidences.

Thorough and permanent life transformations are not generally achieved in the popularized "touch and go" prayer lines for masses of people, or through telecasting a message to millions of viewers. Best results are obtained by "doing what Jesus did", one-on-one. Steady relationships of the young in faith with those deeper in the faith of Christ are a proven way we can trust for individual growth to spiritual maturity.

More than one lesson may be drawn from this case. When young boys and girls are left together unsupervised, they should remain within sight of parents or guardians, and their sleeping arrangements should be substantially separate from each other. Never assume that mixing of the sexes, no matter the blood relationship or age, is protected from active curiosity, lust, or demonic intrusion. Modesty is the standard of Scripture. Holy men pray, while women are to be modest in conduct and apparel (See 1 Timothy 2:8-9). History would have been different had David and Bathsheba observed this rule, which is intended to avert fleshly displays. While modesty has always been the stance for righteous behavior, that principle is magnified in 2 Timothy 3:1 and 13, "This know also, that in the last days perilous times shall come. And verse 13: "But evil men and seducers [male or female] shall wax worse and worse, deceiving, and being deceived." Surely this is that time.

Another lesson is that adults or children with pets often are too enamored with them and are thereby vulnerable to "inordinate affections". Scripture does not enjoin kissing and licking of animals by humans – whether pythons, dogs, horses, et. al. Colossians 3:5: "Mortify … your members which are upon the earth; fornication, uncleanness, inordinate affection, evil concupiscence, and covetousness, which is idolatry". This list of five offenses shows that each one is equally sinful. A single violation may provide advantage to the devil in his attempts to infiltrate the offender's life. Verse 6 adds: "For which things sake [violations] the wrath of God cometh on the children of disobedience. The remedy is to stop doing it – that is, repent.

Emotional ties to beasts - other than for needful services - are often developed as a substitute for failed human relationships. They are the emotional equivalent of addicting one's body to excessive "comfort foods", or drugs such as tobacco products, alcoholic beverages, marijuana, or hard opiates. None of these honors the Lord. Perhaps one's primary emotional attraction to beasts is that most animals are trainable and easy to control. Control of one person over another is forbidden to normal humans. Animals are less intelligent, do not rebuke us, but accept and obey evil masters as readily as righteous ones. They are not judgmental, have no authority over humans. They are helpless to find cures for their diseases, or clean up their vomit and dung, are not morally accountable to anyone. They require as much care as a small child and are expensive to buy and maintain. One can turn on you, as a pet python or a mad dog sometimes does. They can also be inhabited and directed by a demon. Emotional dependency upon a beast of any description is not enjoined in Scripture. Having them for company, for service, or play, however, is not forbidden.

DAVID OF VIOLENCE

We first met on Sunday morning at the church

entrance of Kirkwood Assembly of God. He was leaning against the guardrail. Noting his grim expression, I greeted him with a cheery "Good morning!" He snapped back, "Wutz good about it!?" clearly signaling a problem. I thought bringing relief to this guy would be more important than attending another go-to-church meeting.

I hesitated, and then turned to ask, "How would you like to go with me to a Denny's restaurant? Frankly, I'm hungry and they have pretty good steak and eggs. I'll buy breakfast." He nodded, "OK, yeah," eager but without a smile. We drove the two miles. Ordering the suggested breakfast, we ate, then talked for no less than 12 hours. His need was great.

This began a 17-year relationship. Much could be said, but a central point to be made here is that demons stay with anything dedicated to them and do the most damage when brought into your home, whether we are aware of them or not.

David explained that his immediate problem was that he could not sleep at night. A machinist by trade, exhaustion negatively affected his work. The reason he couldn't get a full night's rest was that the squeaky oven door in his apartment, of itself, repeatedly opened and slammed shut many times each night. He lived alone. Also, there was a continual moaning, and audible footsteps walking back and forth all night long. Covering his ears with a pillow did not help because the evil spirits inside him kept his ears open to the ploys of other demon tormentors in the room.

To look for a cause, we drove to his apartment. Once inside, I saw two paintings hanging on opposite walls that instantly alerted me. One was of an Indian Maharajah squatting in meditations with hands lifted in worship. The other was similar. Already a cause was evident. Walking into the kitchen, I saw two rows of hand-crafted clay idols displayed on a shelf. "Where did you get these, David?" He answered, "My uncle bought them in Peru and gave them to me as a housewarming gift." I explained that these idols and the paintings were the source of his torments. They would have to be destroyed before he could be helped. The Lord warns, "The graven images of their gods shall ye burn with fire: thou shalt not desire the silver or gold that is on them, nor take it unto thee, lest thou be snared therein: for it is an abomination to the Lord thy God. Neither shalt thou bring an abomination into thine house, lest thou be a cursed thing like it: but shalt utterly detest it, and thou shalt utterly abhor it; for it is a cursed thing" (Deuteronomy 7:25-26).

He complained that the idols were a family heirloom, and, as such, he had an emotional attachment to them. Also, "They cost eight thousand dollars!" His family was wealthy. Their mansion was in a posh neighborhood. But now David was being required to decide which was more important—

obtaining peace and health by destroying the idols and paintings, or, keeping the heirlooms and their tormenting demons who could destroy him.

He picked up a hammer and began smashing the idols, promising to throw the residue into the trash the next morning. This he did. Had he refused we would have had no further fellowship. With their destruction, however, peace and rest were restored, and David did well in his employment thereafter. Once again, Scripture informs us those demons have a right to remain with objects either dedicated to them, or that were directly worshiped at some time or place in the world. The requirement for getting the spirits out is to destroy the objects and renounce affiliation with them.

David wondered why he was different from "normal" people who also were born again believers. His life had never been typical. At best, it was exceptional in negative ways. His father was a renowned eye surgeon and professor at a major university and had a staff of servants and a nanny to serve his needs at home. Among the four offspring, David's sister and two brothers were "normal" and well regarded by their father and by society in general. Born mentally retarded, as a young boy David had been institutionalized; insulated and hidden away by his proud father who was embarrassed to claim this son of his. David was shamed, mocked, shunned, hated, left alone, and became obese. There was no chance that he could have a normal education. Normal activities had been tried in earlier years, but that effort only subjected him to further mockery, derision, and failure.

It was clear that he needed serious help in most areas of life. He was then 30 years of age; I was 40. The next seventeen years of our association were bittersweet for me, with numerous tests of patience, endurance, faith, and commitment to his life being rebuilt. It was to be especially challenging, as my wife and I had just founded a formal business and ministry which required our full attention to ensure its survival. David's problems were complicated. Some of them would be resolved as I mentored him over the next decade or so. He was delivered of many demons and shown how to have an acceptable relationship with God and society.

Violent with a demonically inspired death wish, David harbored a hatred of his father which caused him to also hate God as Father. Rage and defiance drove him to race his motorcycle over 100 miles per hour on the aircraft runway at St. Louis International Airport, multiple times! He drove faster than a jet plane! He soon had two wrecks on his two motorcycles. As if that wasn't enough, he also had sky-dived from an airplane more than a hundred times and witnessed his trainer falling to his death after forgetting to put on his parachute.

Instantly realizing he would be dead within the next 60 seconds, he maneuvered fancifully in a show-off.

One time, David sat next to a lady friend on a commercial passenger plane and ended up punching out her teeth during the flight. Another time he similarly punched an elder who was praying for him at the altar of Hegewish Baptist Church, a deliverance church in the South Chicago area. Still another time he threw a pot of hot coffee on Pastor Jim Pigg at Hallelujah House Church. Another time he stood up and publicly "middle-fingered" the preacher during his sermon.

The first time I was to pray for him in my home, we interviewed for a while. At the end, he asked, "What happens if I haul off and slug you while you're praying?" With a daring glare, I replied, "I'll knock your teeth out!" "OK. We understand each other," he said. We did pray, and he was thrown to the floor on his back, as a spirit departed. No punches were thrown.

As to how he might relate to God in the future, I explained that he could forget about his earthly father who always enraged him, as a representation of Father God. "Don't think of God as Father," I said. "Rather, think of Jesus as your brother, your heavenly Father as dead." That was acceptable to him, as he related well to his two brothers.

This ploy was a temporary measure for David

that would keep the channel of teaching open long enough for him to absorb the truth that Father God was not a tyrant like his earthly father. This was a clever "God trick" to defeat the devil, since Jesus informs us, "I and my Father are One" (John 10:30). That is worth a smile! Both David and we should think of Jesus as our elder Brother and Friend (See John 15:14-15).

Numerous public and private deliverances were achieved over the next years. His earthly father died, but his brother Jesus lives on! Our relationship was an example of the partnership of man and God working together. It also reveals that, if man refuses to cooperate, his salvation is aborted. God does not work apart from man, as shown at John 15:5, "Without me ye can do nothing."

That says, "Me and ye", meaning both God and man work together for ministry to be successful. To be sure, this 17-year experience was high adventure.

David admitted that he was different from "normal" believers. I related to his abnormalities, in that much of our lives had been strangely similar. While in process of my own deliverance from demonic intrusions, David's symptoms largely mirrored mine, which made them obvious to me. He had asked "Why can't I be like normal Christians?", whose lives seemed to be blessed in comparison to his.

The answer to his question is twofold. First, it is improper and sad that the prevailing manner of many Christian leaders is to try to homogenize the Lord's flock, as though they could or should become similar, or "normal". What is normal, after all? Each person is unique by design, gifting, and calling, and needs to express his built-in uniqueness.

Second, not everyone is engaged at the same level of warfare. Some have more challenges than others. The Lord has undisclosed reasons for creating such variety. In David's and my own cases, warfare was severe and extended over a long period of time. One theologian describes that reality thus: "There is a fierce and constant conflict between the carnal nature – prone to sin – and the indwelling Holy Spirit."

One day I was enlightened as to how to explain this fact. We were at Denny's Restaurant. Holding up a water glass, I said, "If you take this glass to the edge of Denny's roof top and drop it onto the concrete pavement, it will shatter into hundreds of pieces and shards. While it would be difficult and time-consuming, it might be possible with meticulous care to collect all the pieces and glue them back together. That would somewhat restore the glass to its original shape, but it would be rough and irregular to be sure. That restoration would not make it normal again. A side-by-side comparison of the repaired glass to a new one, would make the differences obvious. The rough, restored one would always appear to be inferior and less desirable. In that way it would be shunned, isolated, and left alone.

"You, David, are that shattered glass—and so am I. God patched us up and brought us together—two of a kind—for fellowship, for ministry to each other and to others like ourselves. We are to minister to those whose lives have been seriously shattered, and to do our best to help glue the pieces back together."

This explanation seemed to hit its mark. His stern face showed that he was straining to grasp the concept, as the word-picture became clearer in his laboring mind. His life slowly improved. Spiritual maturity is not suddenly transplanted but develops by concerted effort over time. David and I similarly are better able to comprehend written paragraphs that are carefully and graphically demonstrated, rather than speedily spoken. We are visual learners. Jesus practiced this principle by demonstration as he "...went about doing good, and healing all that were oppressed of the devil..." (See Acts 10:38; Philippians 4:13; Hebrews 10:9; James 1:22; Romans 2:7; Matthew 7:12). His visible, public, miraculous demonstrations and earthy parables were easy to understand, and their important lessons were thereby learned. Surely it would help people if they could, not only hear words, but also see corresponding miracles demonstrated in the name of Jesus. No one had to guess about the meaning of Jesus' words after seeing His miraculous demonstrations. Ignorant and unbelieving people easily grasp real miracles, even if they cannot read, write, or speak fluently. Let us pray that Christian leaders humble themselves sufficiently to do what Jesus did – that is, demonstrate the whole gospel truth. It was in this way that David's understanding and conduct were slowly restored to full function in most areas of his life over the 17 years of our association. Do you think my time ministering to him was wasted, or spent unwisely? God is never in a hurry. And if David were the only rogue ever saved in human history, Christ's death and resurrection would have been fully justified.

CASE OF THE EBONY MASK

After praying 30 minutes for this lady's deliverance without success, my wife and I determined there was a spiritual obstruction somewhere in the house. We were in the home of then recent acquaintances, Lee and Mary Kerr, a married Christian couple who had attended our seminar. Sitting around their 1950's-style kitchen table, I asked if we could walk through the house together. A spirit of witchcraft seemed to be attached to something. There needed to be a spiritual house cleaning.

Dresser drawers were opened. Various arts, crafts, magazines, trinkets with odd symbols, and photos of owls, frogs and the like, were gathered. Though nothing was instantly conclusive, we applied the rule, "When in doubt, get it out." Collected items were thrown into the black plastic trash bag until it was full.

The last place examined was their master bedroom. On the wall hung a pair of depressed faces carved from ebony wood. Artisans had made them in the Philippine Islands. The couple explained that these were an expensive and meaningful gift from their daughter, who had brought them from her visit to Hawaii. Her parents were understandably hesitant to discard them, but finally decided that deliverance from tormenting demons was more important than keeping replaceable gifts. I explained that artisans often offer such handmade objects to ancestral and other spirits as worship. As prime suspects, the masks were then tossed into the bag of toxic trash.

My wife, Nancy, and I returned to the kitchen and continued praying for Mary. Lee slowly dragged the trash bag from the bedroom, down the hallway, toward the front door. It all had to be removed from the building. As it was towed past us, a demon began to loudly cry out of Mary for the first time. "NO! NO! NO! MASK! MASK! Nooooo! N-o-o-o-o!" At the exact moment the trash was pitched out the door, in one last, prolonged shriek, the demon fled out of Mary and out of the house. What a relief that was! Peace was restored and Mary was delivered. This was additional evidence that demons can and do attach themselves to objects that have been dedicated to them by artisans anywhere in the world. When such dedicated objects are brought into one's residence, the demons remain with the objects, and are thereby enabled to not only wreak havoc, but also enter into the owners who brought them into their abode. See Deuteronomy 7: 25-26 for the biblical explanation of this fact. This is one way in which humans unwittingly become Satan's agents who dispatch demons to other populations.

We became friends with the Lee and Mary family and for years afterward were closely associated in like ministry. Leland was formally ordained to ministry under the oversight of Mission Center International. Together we taught and ministered deliverance in the state of Nebraska and traveled to the states of New Mexico and Georgia on ministry business. They and their son, Ross, conducted weekly deliverance meetings in their home for about 18 years, setting spiritual captives free. Leland was elected a member of our board of directors, until passing into his heavenly home at age 78. Our fellowship with Ross Kerr continues as he ministers deliverance and distributes books to others in Metropolitan St. Louis, Missouri.

Leland had long been a deacon in the Presbyterian Church, even while suffering demonic oppression. Soon after deliverance he opened his home for meetings.

In one notable service a lady, small in stature, was in attendance. She had been deeply immersed in martial arts to the black belt level. When we prayed for the demonic hold upon her to be broken, her strength was supernaturally energized. It required five adult men to hold her down while battling the demons. Though the struggle was intense, the martial arts demons were finally subdued and cast out. Thus we see the source of the brutal martial arts which has since largely dominated a large segment of the sports world.

In Jesus' day, the stigma, opposition, and ugliness of deliverance was more than "respectable preachers" were willing to bear. It remains so today. There probably has never been a time when there was more religion and less of this type of deliverance than now.

PSYCHIC CHIROPRACTOR

A friend recommended that I consult a certain Christian chiropractor to examine my painful back. I knew by experience that the pain was caused by a pinched nerve. Meeting with the doctor was pleasant and his procedure seemed to be in line with that of other doctors. At the conclusion he suggested I return within a week for follow-up, to ensure the adjustment had held. I agreed.

His procedure during the second visit, however, was very different from the first. Instead of the usual twist, he placed his thumbs at the base of my neck and held them with pressure against the brain stem somewhat longer than seemed appropriate. It was the first time such a technique had ever been used on me, and frankly seemed strange. Asked about the technique, he replied that it was one he learned through reading a book written by Dr. Edgar Cayce, a widely publicized psychic healer. He explained that he relied upon the claims made by Edgar Cayce for spiritual healing. Appalled, I determined not to see Dr. David again.

By next morning – still in bed, paralysis had set in. It was so immobilizing and painful that I could not get out of bed. An earlier planned trip with family to Disneyland for that day had to be canceled. Praying most of that day for my own deliverance, the spirit the doctor had imparted into me through his unorthodox psychic procedure was finally defeated. By the next day I was okay—and far wiser! I had been tricked.

About a month passed. Dr. David called me for an appointment for prayer on his behalf. He was suffering under oppression. This would be the second such prayer session at his request. The previous one had been in the office of his pastor, Roland Smith, with whom I was well acquainted. This day he was away on business. It was a bit odd that Dr. David had brought with him a one-gallon glass jug with wide-mouth lid. He said its purpose was for expelling demons into the jug, quickly sealing it, then taking it to a laboratory for analysis. "Surely, something scientific could be learned about demons," he had said. That was quirky foolishness for sure, and humorous.

The prayer session was to take place in my home. Associate Gus Mackris, an able minister, was present to assist. (Gus and I, together in prayer, had once lengthened a man's lame leg nearly one and a half inches – Gus at his feet and I at his head. The gritty bone crunching in the process was audible!)

Due to the earlier paralysis experience generated by Dr. David's psychic thumb procedure, I required something of him before prayer would begin.

"Doctor," I admonished, "before we can pray in good conscience for your deliverance, you will have to both renounce the psychic spirit that operates through you and stop using the techniques of Doctor Edgar Cayce. Further, you must destroy all his books in your possession. Perhaps you are not aware how damaging your treatments are when using his techniques; they actually paralyzed me one full day. Are you willing to commit to this requirement?"

Dr. David bristled at the idea, saying, "That would destroy my practice and my income! I would have to go out of business. No, I cannot commit to it."

That sounded conclusive. To his final comment, I

replied, "Since that is your decision, I have no faith to believe you would be helped by our prayers. Unless and until you meet the conditions for deliverance, you will remain in your demonic torment. There is no further need to spend more time on this. This meeting is adjourned."

With that, he walked out of my home a disappointed and disgruntled man.

One time later we accidentally saw each other in a public service at the Hallelujah House Church, nodding but not voicing acknowledgment of each other. It was the last time I saw him. He died at age 92.

The point is, demons are attached to items, literature, and books which testify of their work in some measure, and they legally remain wherever the items are kept. Their job description is the same as their boss'—steal, kill, and destroy. Never give or donate such items to anyone—no matter how expensive they may be. If you don't want their demons, why would you open the door for someone else to fall victim to them?

If you want the demons out of your life, throw out their things. Better yet, destroy their stuff with fire—the ultimate destruction. If the items won't burn, smash them. Render them useless. One time a Ouija board was cast into a flaming fireplace; its demon screamed out of the flames! This was testified by Dr.

Charles Jarman, who, interestingly, had pastored and preached the gospel 52 years before he was saved!

This principle includes printed literature and the reading of horoscopes, whether taken seriously or not. These are deceptions from the deceiver, and their readers may be brought under serious bondage. For information about your present and future status in this regard, go to the original Source and ask. The Lord knows everything about you before, during, and after your life on earth. Read Deuteronomy 18:10-12. "Observer of times" is the reading of horoscopes. Stop reading them.

DESTROYER OF RELATIONSHIPS

Bonnie was a realtor who sold me four out-of-state houses as rental investments. Over the months of our business relationship, I learned that she was a 32 years-old mother of a 16 years-old son and had never been married. She explained that several times a serious relationship with suitors had developed, but each time, when marriage seemed eminent, something happened that was unexplainable, ending the prospect of marriage. She couldn't understand why.

An avid reader, she agreed to read books I selected and sent to her, which explained the reality, work, and deliverance from demons. She was of the Catholic faith. By the time of my next trip to her town, she had read the books and was ready and willing to receive prayer. After her office staff had left for the day, I gave final instructions, and she made her confession of believing on the Lord Jesus Christ. We began our typical prayer in the knowledge of what to expect; we engaged the demon, identifying him as Destroyer of Relationships, commanding him to depart from her. A secondary spirit of lust manifested by stretching out and stiffening her fingers, which is a common manifestation of that spirit. More directly, however, we wanted to break the hold of the primary spirit who kept destroying her relationships with men who expressed their love and wanted to marry her. Within half an hour that spirit's hold was broken and it was cast out. Six months later, she married an attorney from Florida and the next year gave birth to a beautiful girl. To celebrate the deliverance victory, she named her daughter Victoria! She sent a greeting card, which lauded me as her pastor. How sweet and endearing that was, though we were residents of different states 700 miles apart. She received her miracle, fulfilling the desire of her heart. God is good, and faithful to all who genuinely call upon Him for help, no matter the nature of the need.

ARLENE, LOIS AND SCIENTOLOGY

Our meeting with Lois came about through Arlene, who had recently been set free from five demons, occasioned in our office at Bible Voice, Inc. The latter's main bondage had been a spirit of gluttony—the strong man of the group. Others were lust, sloth, fear, and hate.

She had been morbidly obese and slovenly. That deliverance was notable and memorable for three reasons: 1) It was my first solo ministry in casting out demons. 2) The Holy Spirit anointing had amazed me by mightily showing up in extraordinary manifestation of faith and power. Just the raising of my hands caused exaggerated demonic reactions. 3) The strongman, Gluttony, fought fiercely for a time after the others had been evicted, but finally succumbed in screaming so loudly that my secretary in another office became alarmed and phoned the president of the company to tell him "all about it". I was ecstatic that the Lord's seal had thereby been set upon me for this new aspect of ministry.

Reporting back two weeks later, Arlene had lost 35 pounds! She said she was horrified when, for the first time, she was able to clearly see how utterly junky and messy her house was. It had been so bad that her husband separated from her by reason of the mess of both the house and her gluttonous body. Before the deliverance, she had been demoniacally prevented from seeing it through her clouded eyes.

Excited in her new freedom, she asked if my wife and I would minister at her Pentecostal church in South Los Angeles. We agreed, and after the teaching, we gave an altar call for any who had need of deliverance. The lone lady who responded was Lois. That might not seem to be an enthusiastic response, but it turned out that she alone was all we could handle over the next four hours!

The daughter of missionaries, Lois had been raised in China. As is typical, certain constraints were imposed upon her for proper behavior there, requiring discipline and tolerance toward a culture foreign to her, and privation from typical privileges in mainland America. Over time, resentment developed, and she began to read Dianetics: The Modern Science of Mental Health, a book by L. Ron Hubbard, founder of the Church of Scientology. Its principal adherents are intellectuals and Hollywood movie actors, prominent among whom is actor Tom Cruise, as widely publicized.

The combination of resentment and turning from Christ to an intellectual religious system opened her to an invasion by demons. There was no tape recording of the deliverance event as my wife, Nancy, and I ministered.

While helping me, however, Nancy intermittently was able to write sketchy notes of the deliverance dialogue, which are now before me. A spirit of lust was the first to speak. He proudly proclaimed, "I've been living inside her a long time—twelve years! The blood of Jesus isn't strong enough to make me go! I'm not afraid of the name of Jesus—or the blood of Jesus!" He was bragging like a paper tiger.

Responding to my inquiry the spirit answered, "Her mind is the stronghold."

Then another spirit named himself: "Gluttony. Sweet things. Chocolate with nuts. Don't like people touching me—especially men."

At age 2, Lois had briefly returned to America, where she had eaten an entire box of chocolate candy to satisfy her pent-up craving.

Demon: "I'm in the sinus, too. I am not coming out!

Jesus isn't strong enough! He's only a man."

Next Demon: "Fear—strong man. Everything is against me—twelve years."

Demon: "Pain and Anxiety. Fear of Rejection—afraid of everything and everybody."

Demon: "Self-Attraction. Self-Pity—twelve years." Demon: "Dianetics—in the mind—fingers on the mind.

I'm not going into dry places.

Yakity Yak! I have strong bands—she's playing around with religion. Very delicate!"

Demon: "Rebellion. I'm against authority. Had witchcraft for 2000 years. Twelve years. I'm not compromising, either! I want her soul! I have long fingers around the cerebellum - like a mat in the brain. I don't like praise."

Demon: Confusion— "mind is not clear."

I commanded: "Bow before the name of Jesus!"

Demon: "Never done it before! I was an angel of light — sent to destroy the mind of Lois. I have a finger on the cranium, hooked under the eyes!"

Demon: "Dianetics, I operate at the subconscious level."

This was a difficult deliverance. My wife and I persisted until two o'clock in the morning, long after the teaching had concluded. Though the dialogue is incomplete here, the ministry was significant and successful. It is sufficient to point out the danger of embracing the religious system called Scientology.

My experience with Lois' involvement in this demonic cult occurred in 1971. Since then, Scientology has spread exponentially and is reportedly a billion-dollar religious institution. In 2016-17 an expose' of its all-encompassing bondage of adherents has repeatedly been presented on the A&E Television Network under the title "Scientology & the Aftermath." It was produced by widely known actress, Leah Remini, who had succumbed to its deceptive control over 27 years and promoted it. Her eye-opening presentation does not consider the demonic impetus that propels the religion, but the facts she reveals of her captivity clearly proves one thing: Scientology is a pernicious work of Satan to be avoided. Demons drive it and enter into some of its adherents.

There are terrible consequences for dabbling in occult religions, their branches, or instruments—which are many and far-reaching. See Deuteronomy 28:14-68 for the Lord's roster of curses imposed for turning to "other gods".

One of the most common door openers for demons is the reading of horoscope. It is firmly forbidden in Deuteronomy 18:10-19, expressed there as "Observer of times". A companion offense is the reading or study of astrology (horoscope) and playing with the so-called children's game, Ouija board, which operates by demonic maneuvering of letters or numbers to answer questions put to it. Through its use, demons often enter and victimize the child. The rule to heed is: anything supernatural that bypasses the Lord Jesus Christ is of demonic origin and must be avoided.

CASE OF AN ORTHODOX JEW

This case involves two occasions of a lady's deliverance from demons. What sets it apart from most others is that she was an orthodox Jew who did not believe that Jesus Christ is the Messiah of the Jews. In spite of that, she received major deliverance from Jesus in disguise. Meeting her was ostensibly because of the For Sale sign in her yard, near where I was looking for a house to buy. Our discussions soon turned from the subject of real estate to her employment. She said she was a counselor in the field of physical therapy. I replied that I also was a counselor. Her next question was, "What kind? I replied, "Exorcism". She was instantly eager to know more. We made an appointment to meet the next day to discuss the subject. With open Bible I began to show scriptures in the "Jewish half" of the Bible. One reveals the plurality of the One God. At no time did I mention the name Jesus. Doing so would have put up a barrier, realizing she did not believe the New Testament account of the messianic Jesus. Her resistance to Christianity's Jesus had been reinforced by historical persecution of Jews by Gentiles, whom God used to pass judgment for their denial and persecution of Messiah. Fortunately, she trusted in the words of the Old Testament. Thus, I began by pointing her to appropriate Old Testament scriptures. We discussed their prophetic fulfillment and application to deliverance from demonic powers, over our four hours in Coco's restaurant booth, five miles from her house. The main scriptures shown were:

Genesis 1:26 "God" in this verse is Elohim, which, in Hebrew is plural. "And God said, Let US make man in OUR image, after OUR likeness."

Psalm 22:8 and 16 "He trusted on the LORD that

he would deliver him: let him deliver him, seeing that he delighted in him."

16 "For dogs have compassed me: the assembly of the wicked have enclosed me: they pierced my hands and my feet."

Zechariah 13:6 "And one shall say unto him, what are these wounds in thine hands? Then he shall answer, Those with which I was wounded in the house of my friends."

Isaiah 52:14"…his visage was so marred more than any man, and his form more than the sons of men." These verses describe the future suffering, death, and character of the Messiah, all of which were fulfilled by Jesus.

After rehearsing these prophesies, she suddenly blurted out: "I'm ready!" Surprised at the fast work of the Old Testament Scripture, I was nonetheless pleased. Though we had not discussed Jesus by name, she wanted immediate prayer for deliverance from demonic torments – through Old Testament provisions alone. But where could we go for such an engagement? We had already worn out our welcome in the restaurant booth. Then I remembered a rental house two miles north. The tenants were away at work and in school. I said, "Follow me to my Copperwood house; we can pray there."

She sat in a chair while I rehearsed the prayer and the procedure we would follow. She agreed.

Here is the really fascinating part. Not once would I mention the name Jesus, even as I appealed to Him to set her free from demonic powers. This was to be an important lesson and revelation.

Though the Lord is highly jealous of his holy name and how it is to be used, He regards a lady's deliverance more important than any formula of prayer. He looks upon our heart, not on the outward appearance (I Samuel 16:7). Furthermore, his Spirit works equally well on either side of the cross. That is, before or after Jesus' birth, death and resurrection. Scripture says of the Lord, "I change not" (Malachi 3:6). Also, "whosoever shall call upon the [Old or New Testament, direct or indirect] name of the Lord shall be delivered" [Joel 2:32 and Acts 2:21].

After preliminary explanation, I laid my right hand on her forehead, while raising up the left in honor of the Lord, and commanded, "Satan, I come against you in the name of the God of Abraham, Isaac, and Jacob! I command you and your demons to loose this daughter of Abraham" (See Luke 13:16).

I named a battery of unclean spirits and other kindred spirits, demanding that they leave her. Instantly they reacted. Their screams were so loud and protracted that I was concerned the neighbors would call the police to investigate the scene. None came. I was relieved to remember that the neighbors were still away at work and at school. There were about 15 demons expelled within 90 minutes. She became a remarkably changed woman from that time forward.

I bought her house, and we remained in contact. Two months after her deliverance, I returned to her town where we again met in a restaurant. After two hours of further Bible study, this lady declared she would now and in future worship and serve the Lord Jesus Christ as her Messiah. She had learned that Jesus Christ, whether by Old or New Testament identification, had always been God and Savior. She had unwittingly worshiped Him under Old Testament laws all along. Ever present from the time of Creation, He became known as The God of Abraham, Isaac, and Jacob," as effectively, reverently, and truly as by the later name and title, The Lord Jesus Christ. His power that parted the Red Sea for Israel has continued to manifest throughout history and shall to infinity. This lady's second deliverance was recorded on audio cassette.

Among her problems had been divorce from her husband after he and his father had repeatedly molested her daughter sexually over four years beginning at age five. Both men had been sentenced to prison for their crimes. The first deliverance of this lady had been substantial, but incomplete. During our second meeting, she asked for more and specific prayers. The first ten minutes of the prayers the second time seemed to have no effect. But a telltale movement from deep below her abdomen gave me pause. It wasn't a reaction that was expected. I asked, "Have you had an abortion"? She replied, "Yes. How did you know?" This wasn't the time to explain at length. We now had to shift the procedure and deal with the core hindrance to any further deliverance. The strong man spirits of murder and death were deeply entrenched. Unless they were removed there could be no further progress. Abortion presupposes a willful, long-premeditated murder – the extreme expression of Satan: self-will, selfishness, in defiance of the will of God. John 8:44 explains that "He was a murderer from the beginning". That fact is reinforced in John 10:10: "The thief [Satan] cometh not, but for to steal, and to kill, and to destroy."

Our renewed effort to set her free now required that she confess her sin of murder, renounce the demons of murder and death, who by reason of abortion-murder, had been given legal right to enter into her. She also had to truly and profoundly repent of the attitude that had caused her problem. After she complied, we battled 81 minutes to gain her freedom. The tape recording made of this event shows the depth of the struggle. It was not pretty but was successful.

The worldwide industry that mass-murders babies – 60 million in the USA – is a holocaust much greater than those perpetrated by the three most celebrated dictators of the twentieth century combined - Mao Zedong, Adolph Hitler, and Josef

Stalin. Masses of children are being sacrificed to the false god of selfishness. This is parallel to ancient Israel and heathen nations sacrificing their children on the altar fires of the demon gods of Canaan. Nothing could be more abominable. Read of it in Psalm 106:25-43, the books of I Kings, I Thessalonians 2:14-16, 2 Chronicles, and elsewhere in the Holy Bible.

No person or nation is exempt from divine punishment for willful wickedness.

Genuine Christian policy and practice from the beginning has been to love and serve Abrahamic Gentiles and Israeli Jews alike. Romans 2:11: "For there is no respect of persons with God." As a closing side note, it has been my privilege to minister deliverance to only a few men and women of Israel. One was a ranking major in the Israeli Defense Forces (IDF) All were introduced to their Messiah, and one man was elected to our Mission Center International board of directors and served well until the time of his death.

CASE OF MANY VOICES

"Many voices have gone out into the world and none of them is without significance" (I Corinthians 14:10 paraphrased). These include thought-voices spoken by good or evil spirits.

Thoughts are the voices of spirits without sound. Expressing them out loud requires the use of human vocal cords, which may be spoken variously in soft, comforting tones, as well as with guttural, demanding torments.

Without thought-voices being introduced and processed the human mind would be useless to either oneself or to good or evil spirits. The Holy Spirit, however, generally speaks to our human spirit, but at the same time, may also enlighten our mind.

In nearly all cases of demonic influence, whether from inside or outside the body, an individual remains fully functional most of the time in every normal way. Aberrations and dysfunction progressively worsen when the victimized person is not aware that his affliction is of demonic origin. Intermittent episodes of destructive thoughts range from subtle, to moderate, to severely debilitating. The latter may be diagnosed as insanity and become permanent unless their real source is discovered, and the demon cast out.

In this lady's case all these conditions were in evidence during our several meetings. The compulsive voices that first guided, then drove her, were constant and convincing. She believed and acted upon their lies. Her life was a shambles in finances, relationships, and emotional distress. She was an unwed mother on parole, living in a state-sponsored community house, had no transportation, little clothing, and no spiritual guidance.

As I taught her out of the Holy Bible, she quickly showed interest in the better things of life. But during and after each session the voices kept telling her the information, she was hearing was fraudulent, and that she had to obey her "inner voices". In our final session the power of the demons would be crushed. The occasion of this deliverance was on the worst afternoon of her life. She was literally "out of her mind" with multiple demons yelling names inside her mind – but not aloud through her mouth. She was in serious distress, stuttered, and wrote several names on my note paper. It was difficult for me to write the names being stuttered. There were too many. I said, "Here, you write them", handing her my clipboard and ink pen. She wrote two columns of about 24-30 names, as they were barked in her mind. The names were of her close friends, in-laws, relatives – essentially all her nearest associates, such as might be on her email address book.

They were forceful, involuntary torments. The demons had surveilled her movements, actions, and social contacts sufficiently to have them catalogued. They were well mimicked as familiar voices of her friends. Together the group of them convinced her to believe, obey and act upon their instructions – exactly contrary to the Scriptures I quoted to her.

All the voices – theirs and mine – were equally strong and influential. Theirs would tell her, "He is lying to you. Do not believe him; he cannot be trusted. You know us. He is wrong; you know we are right. Your friends would not lie to you. Ignore him."

I had taken her to a church bookstore where she selected a monogrammed Holy Bible, which I purchased as a gift to her. It was the promises God has given to believers that the demons were telling her were lies, and not to read or believe them. Amid her tears and uncertainty, she repeatedly turned her head, first to "them" and alternately to me. Now angry, I determined to stop them. Opening the bottle of anointing oil, I anointed her head with oil, and forcefully commanded the voices to stop speaking, and quoted the verses of James 5:14-15, "Is any sick among you? Let him call for the elders of the church and let them pray over him, anointing him with oil in the name of the Lord: and the prayer of faith shall save the sick, and the Lord shall raise him up...". "Now, you lying, tormenting demons – on the authority of these words of God, by the anointing of the Holy Spirit, as an elder in the Church of Jesus Christ, I command you to shut your mouth, line up in order, and come out of her. Right now, get up and get out!"

Frankly, I was a little surprised that they didn't put up a fight. I had expected some screaming and violent resistance, as had often been so in other deliverances. How glad I was! The Lord was especially gracious and merciful. In years past, I had expended a great amount of physical energy in such cases but was now being shown that such strenuous efforts would no longer be necessary. It had been good training. Now the "faith of the Son of God" would operate through His word and Spirit with "less of me and more of Him". Thank you, Lord! In just a few moments this lady was delivered, set free from her demonic torments. All was quiet – inside and outside.

Here is my editorial: You may think or ask how it comes about that I meet people with so much need. Let me not be arrogant or simplistic in answering. Honestly, I do not seek out people with "special needs". Everyone has such a need to a lesser or greater extent. "They"/we are everywhere. The person you meet in church is there for only one reason; he or she has a need. That is true of customers or staff in restaurants, workplaces, apartment residences, friends, and relatives.

Most modern churches appear to be religious "half-way houses". They neither teach nor practice deliverance from demons, and carefully avoid Bible teachings and demonstrated precedents by Jesus and his disciples. Apostasy has become so prevalent and insidious that I no longer know of a church or pastor to recommend for this kind of help. Advertised telephone prayer lines on television are of some help but are woefully insufficient to meet the in-person needs. The same is true of many fellowship meetings, "addiction" phone counseling, etc. All are of some help but often mix fund-raising with prerecorded generic prayers. They are "social distancing" from people's deepest needs.

On-screen smiley faces and voices of comfort are okay. Elementary level Bible teaching and the eloquent telling of others' stories is inspiring and informative. A friendly congregational pat on your shoulder by the one sitting next to you expresses sympathy. When you return next week you may have the same experience, and over the weeks and years after that, also. Such touches are the most popular and tepid "form of godliness" (2 Timothy 3:5), but the messy work of the hard gospel is thereby left to others, if and when such a rare another can be found. Pastors must both teach and demonstrate the whole gospel. How else can their flock first become free of bondage, then likewise do the same "work of the ministry" to destroy the works of the devil (1 John 3:8 and John 14:12). Everyone is to do it.

What, then, are we to do? We are to adopt the attitude and be taught that we are soldiers at war; it is not peace time. Do all that you know is right to do. Pray, fast, read the Scripture promises of God for your good. Pay the Lord His tithe. Call for help. Fellowship with Christian believers. Repent of all known sinful conduct. Be honest, keep all your promises, pay your bills. Do not keep company with unbelievers. Follow and perform the Scripture precedents.

Trust in the word of God: "Finally, my brethren, be strong in the LORD, and in the power of his might. Put on the whole armour of God, that ye may be able to stand against the wiles of the devil. For we wrestle not against flesh and blood, but against principalities, against powers, against the rulers of the darkness of this world, against spiritual wickedness in high places. Wherefore take unto you the whole armor of God, that ye may be able to withstand in the evil day, and having done all, to stand" (Ephesians 6:10-13).

Gathering of information by demons who surveil us is clearly shown in two deliverance cases in BOOK ONE. In Patty's case, one demon said to Derek Prince, "I followed you all over – for five years." That was in Kenya and other nations.

In the case of the demonized teenage boy under the ministry of Norman Parish, multiple demons repeatedly followed and ran ahead of him to his stated destination in their effort to stop and kill him. They were sent by overlords in witchcraft centers, and after concluding their failed attempts, reported back to their headquarters for further instructions.

In the case of this lady, the demons had gathered all her personal contact information to use against her. Satan's followers – all demons and many humans – gain access to all your personal information, as well as knowledge of your circle of friends and relatives. As Scripture says, "And a man's foes shall be they of his own household" (Matthew 10:36), and "The wicked watcheth the righteous, and seeketh to slay him" (Psalm37:32). We can hardly afford to be anything but diligent in protecting personal information and contacts who can and will be used against us.

DR. GLEN PhD

Spiritual and circumstantial problems combine in a unique mix for each person. There are markers, however, that are typical of a great many people. This gentleman had telephoned from South Dakota. An appointment was made for our meeting in Oklahoma. Our face-to-face interview revealed his inward, spiritual characteristics as well as their outward expressions. The inward items were common, as revealed in the Holy Bible. The outward manifestation of his demon-caused characteristics, however, were unusual. An apparently unlikely relationship between an effect and its cause is a useful strategy employed in both military and spiritual armies. The purpose in using a diversionary tactic is to deceive one's enemy. So-called damaging accidents are not accidental, but are evil plans well executed. In this understanding I treat every negative event or condition, first as demon inspired, and secondarily as something more logical and apparent.

Demon-inspired events usually are initiated subsurface and invisible, but from start to finish they are no less real than are the Rocky Mountains.

Glen's ostensible purpose in driving a thousand miles through several states to keep our appointment was to discuss his possible purchase of our for-sale business. That did not happen. The divine purpose was to grant him a deliverance miracle. Though he was intelligent and had earned a doctorate degree from a Christian university, he had not been taught the basics of deliverance from demons. Here are the names of his tormentors whom we dealt with, and some of the physical symptoms caused by one named "Allergies".

INWARD CHARACTERISTICS

- Mental Confusion, Indecision, Impotence
- Ahab
- Double Minded, Antisocial
- Fear, Shy, Timid

OUTWARD CHARACTERISTICS

- Allergies
- Chill - Cold Ears
- Stiff Neck (from use of colognes)
- Shaky Voice/Spasm Lower Back pain (from use of hair gels)

This deliverance was different from most where I had officiated. There seemed to be no logical relationship between the spirits and their outward expressions. There was no direct prayer command given to a specific spirit, and no laying on of hands.

Instead, together we declared a Spiritual Warfare Decree on behalf of himself, his family, and property. I gave him a printed copy to keep and to post in his home.

He departed that same evening. An hour later he called to report his location: Bartlesville, Oklahoma.

While he was driving, the demons became active and began to flee out of him one after the other. This was the result of the two of us agreeing in prayer, declaring out loud all the points of the Warfare Decree. That was our part to do. The LORD's part was to honor our faith. He always does.

For every reader's benefit, the referenced DECREE has been reprinted in this book. As you read it, I encourage you to declare its provisions for yourself and your family. Just as others have seen the answer to their prayer, expect the Lord to answer your appeal also. God is faithful to hear and to answer honest prayers. In doing so, I am confident that you will be amazed at the result.

CHAPTER THREE

MENTAL AND PHYSICAL DELIVERANCE

There are Christian ministers who teach that demons do not exist. That notion contradicts Scripture, the teachings of Jesus, biblical evidence, the practice of the apostles, and ordinary believers who still cast demons out of believers. Others believe in part but pretend that Satan's influence on Christians has been all but eradicated. Meanwhile, demons are "chewing them up and spitting them out" through a thousand diseases, moral failings, imprisonment for crimes they commit, and dying early death. By ignoring the facts, their congregations and television viewers fare no better.

Is there a quick fix for this mayhem? Yes, and no. The yes part is that leaders could begin believing and acting upon the part of Jesus' gospel most disgusting to them, i.e. casting demons out of victims in their congregations. That alone would quickly begin to turn the tide against Satan's freedom to weaken and cripple untaught believers almost at will.

This cannot be accomplished through television. However, such an obedience would fulfill Jesus' statement, "Greater works than these shall he do in (my name) because I go to my Father" (John 14:12).

The "no" part of the answer is that the extreme comfort of those who comprise the Christian hierarchy will not be sacrificed. The ruling class continues their rule by compromising the whole gospel. Congregations generally follow their leaders. Thus, the satanic mayhem has continued unopposed for the most part. This ongoing dilemma is clearly affirmed in Apostle Paul's declaration: (2 Timothy 4:3-4) "For the time will come when they will not endure sound doctrine; but after their own lusts shall heap to themselves teachers, having itching ears. (4) And they shall turn away their ears from the truth and shall be turned unto fables." Though repugnant to some, the wondrous part of the gospel addressed here glares from the pages of the Holy Bible. Matthew 10:7, Mark 16 and Luke 10:19-20 are confirmed in Matthew 28:18-20. The truth of those passages was given as the last and great commission by Jesus, just before he ascended into heaven. Should teachers and preachers ignore his commands? Never, if one is a truly believing leader.

TESTIMONY OF RUSS PILCHER

"Our daughter came to a point in life where she was oppressed of the devil. She was walking in the Holy Spirit, and we visited her often. We talked on the telephone at length, and I had a great deal of inner turmoil about her entertaining the notion of evil spirits tormenting her. I was raised in the Missouri Synod Lutheran Church, and they were about as stiff-necked as anybody. This just did not register in my spirit because Lutherans had not taught that subject in the Missouri Synod Church. I believed initially that anyone who had professed Christ and given his life to Him, there was no way he could have a demon spirit and I stated it to my daughter vehemently.

"One morning I was praying after talking to her the previous night. She had called me expressing joy over being delivered of two or three demons that evening. Driving to work next morning, I was greatly disturbed that she was "off" into error. I had not slept well. I earnestly prayed to the Lord, asking that He reveal to me whether her claim was true or not. While driving I burst into tears, and suddenly a great peace came over me. The Lord answered, "This is true." That showed me that life-long Christians – even after being baptized in the Holy Spirit – can most certainly have demon spirits indwelling them. He impressed on me that this ministry was truly okay. What they were doing was all right. Truly excited, I could hardly wait to get to work and call my wife to tell her about this, because she was troubled too. I do not think it is uncommon that "old school" Christians are uneasy with this teaching. I think the teaching is more prevalent today because the Lord has once again awakened people to request His Baptism of the Holy Spirit. One of the works of the Holy Spirit is to teach or remind us of the things Jesus said while on earth. What is happening now is that the body of true believers is being jarred out of complacency and coming more alive in the Lord to make these things happen. But it is real. It is true. It is the Word of God."

It needs to be understood, however, that no true believer can be fully "possessed" by demons, which implies ownership. Creator God is Owner and "prime minister".

An analogy here might help our understanding of this concept. If a hundred-room hotel has one or two rooms occupied by someone evil does not mean the other rooms are empty. Other rooms house good tenants. So it is with a Christian's personality. Satanic agents can occupy one or two rooms - as many as they can, but they can never take over the hotel because the Spirit of God is Owner and Chief Resident. In previous pages we explained aspects of the human spirit, soul, and body. When we are born-again, our human spirit is regenerated by the

Holy Spirit, forever belonging to God. But the soul area, the flesh area, the carnal nature, the mind, will, intellect, emotions - the whole personality is the spiritual battleground and the source of our troubles.

The word "possessed", as translated from Greek in the King James English should correctly be "demonized". A person is either influenced by an evil spirit or he is not. It is only a matter of degree because everyone is sometimes oppressed of the devil in some way. Some differentiate between inside or outside the body. That is not the key issue. The main matter is that, when we are oppressed of the devil, we need to get the oppression removed. If an evil spirit is discovered inside, get him out. The intensity, duration and diagnosis of a problem will lead us to the correct conclusion.

Many wonder who Jesus was talking about in Mark 16:16-17 when he commanded "they shall cast out demons". It is important to know the answer. The overriding Scripture is, "He that believeth and is baptized shall be saved; but he that believeth not shall be damned." Here we see that whoever is not a believer is already damned. Every one of us is in one of the only two categories. There is no other option. Which category are you in? Are you saved? Do you truly believe in Jesus Christ? Now let us read verse 17. "And these signs shall follow them that believe; In my name shall they cast out devils; [The word 'devils' should rightly be translated "demons", as there is only one devil. There should not properly be degrees or varieties of believing. It is vital to know that each and all believers are included under this command. Jesus is saying, "You shall cast out demons" in His name. That task is not to be left for somebody else to do. You may think that only some well-known minister is supposed to do it. That would be an error. It really says believers like you and me shall perform these signs. "...In My name they [you] shall cast out demons, they [you] shall speak with new tongues." There are other things that you will do also. The Lord says, "These signs... will follow you if you believe. If you are saved, you shall do these things: if you accidentally pick up a snake and are bitten, or otherwise poisoned in performance of the Lord's commands, the Lord says it will not hurt you. He also says you prayerfully will lay hands on the sick and they shall recover from the sickness. Recover implies a process of healing but may include a miracle of instant healing as well. This does not mean that the moment you are born-again you immediately are placed into a full-time faith and preaching ministry. That may or may not be your divine gift. Nearly always there first is a time of learning to embrace the main doctrines of the Christian faith. You learn that you have been saved by the power of God because someone told you the good news that Jesus Christ voluntarily died the death you deserved. You were born into the kingdom of God in spirit, but it does not mean that you, still a novice, should immediately begin a full-time ministry to preach the gospel. It also does not mean that you should immediately try to perform every one of these signs that shall follow mature believers. The first twelve disciples had been personally taught three years by Jesus in word and deed, closely observing all that he did and how he did it. They were not sent forth as novices. While a long learning process is the typical pattern for us to follow, it is not an invariable rule. God makes exceptions as he sees fit.

For example, our church hosted a number of recently delivered and converted drug addicts in Chicago. They publicly referred to themselves as "The Addicts." We sponsored a home for them for a time. God would deliver these fellows from the power of the devil and drugs. Within a week or so, they would bring other drug addicts into this house, lay hands on them, pray for them, and cast out demons. Those young people were quickly being healed by God working through new babes in Christ! This is one type of exception but is not a rule for every novice to follow. You need to know that if you will believe these words of the Lord Jesus Christ and act on them, even in blind, dumb obedience, you will find such things happening under your own hands! You will lengthen lame legs. You will cast out demons. You will cure them by the laying on of your hand, claiming it in Jesus' name. It is you who will do that! Astonishing? Yes, but true. You may think, "Who, me? Who am I? I've only been two years in the faith."

The devil speaks lies in your mind, such as "Your prayer doesn't mean that much because, after all, look at your background. Who are you to be praying for others?" Ignore him! Pray! Take action on behalf of someone who needs help. Satan hates rightly motivated prayers because he knows those prayers will be answered. He aims to stop you with excuses. A father may say, "I want you to pray for my daughter. She's hooked on drugs. She's out in the world and lost to the devil." His heart is crying out. He says it before a gathering of 30 believers. Whereupon the devil goes to each one and says, "Who are you to pray for that girl? Look at your life. You don't have time. You're too busy. Don't waste your time. You can breathe a prayer, but don't get too excited about it. You have enough on your plate; don't add to your burden. People should be praying for you instead of you praying for others. Who are you to pray for some girl lost out there? You don't even know her. Besides, there are 29 others already praying for her."

One at a time, Satan tries to pick us off with lying words of discouragement. He exploits our weaknesses and sometimes our strengths. If he can get you alone, away from the flock, he can talk you down. That is the battle we face. But that is the time to call him a liar, stand on the Word of God, and begin proclaiming, "Devil, listen to me. The Lord says, "By the blood of the Lamb and the word of my testimony I overcome you. The Bible says I am seated in heavenly places with Christ Jesus. I walk in the power of the Lord Jesus Christ under the anointing of the Holy Spirit. Jesus Christ defeated you at the cross of Calvary. He gave me power and authority and dominion over you, and nothing shall by any means hurt me because I am a child of God, while you are a liar and the father of lies. I therefore intercede on behalf of that girl. Hallelujah! I remit her sins unto God. And the Lord says in John 20:23, "Whose soever sins ye remit, they are remitted unto them". I remit her sins unto Christ! I claim her for the kingdom of God! I speak words of life and truth to her. Hallelujah. I thank God for bringing her into the kingdom of God. And Satan, I rebuke you in the name of the Lord. I command you to take your hands off that girl, in Jesus' mighty name!" No matter if that girl is a thousand miles away or across the ocean. The Word of God is not hindered by human perceptions of distance or time because God is everywhere at all times.

Here is a personal example. Once I was in Detroit for three days on business, and under conviction of sin. Though I had first come to the Lord at eight years of age, I strayed away at age twelve and denied God for decades. There I was in the Dorchester Motel on Grand River Drive on January 17, weary of boozing whiskey. It was the night after my birthday. Looking out the front door, wondering where to go for the evening, suddenly there appeared in my mind, "Why don't you read the Bible?" It was like a lighted sign. How strange that thought was after all my years of ignoring the Lord! I had no understanding of where thoughts came from at that time in my life. In ignorance I believed only what I personally knew and could see. Every thought that occurred in my mind was mine, and there had never been an occasion to question it.

God was up to something. I did not know until months later, while visiting my brother, Danny, in St. Louis, that he had written my name on a piece of paper and tacked it onto a prayer board in that little storefront church on South Jefferson Avenue. It was on that very same night— January 17. That little congregation—just a handful of people at Faith Tabernacle—prayed over the name David Keklikian. Six hundred miles away, God instantly answered their prayer so that these words flashed into my mind: "Why don't you read the Bible?" That began a fantastic chain of events leading me to who I am today. I was so impressed with what I read that I stole the Gideon Bible from that room and read it the next 18 months! Later, of course, I more than repaid the Gideons for that stolen Bible. It is a wonderful example that shows even simple prayers are powerful. Not only are they important, but they will also change people's lifestyle and their destiny from hell to heaven.

The Bible teaches, "If My people which are called by my name, shall humble themselves, and pray, and seek my face, and turn from their wicked ways; then will I hear from heaven, and will forgive their sin, and will heal their land" (2 Chronicles 7:14).

If there is any land on earth that needs healing today, it is your land! Who is God talking about there? It is not to only a few geographic locations. No. "If my people…." any place in the world. He is not making that promise to the devil's crowd destined for hell. The most fantastic privilege possible is that of being called to salvation. Therefore, praying is no small thing. It is the most important thing you can do. "Praying always…" (Ephesians 6:18).

Satan continues to speak negative thoughts in your mind. You must know your position in Christ, stand on the Word of God, and tell Satan to go "jump in the lake" - the one that burns with fire and brimstone—because that is to be his permanent home.

These signs will follow you because you believe. You will cast out demons and you can declare it to the devil. But you have to take a hard line against him. You have to love the needy person while being hard against the demon ruling him. Demons never run just because you talk to them. The Bible has not instructed us to engage in conversation or to give them options. Instead, it says, "They shall cast out demons."

A type of casting out a demon is pictured in a belligerent drunkard sitting at a bar. The bartender tries to be nice and accommodating: "Hey Charlie, don't ya think it would be better for you to go home now? Your wife and kids are waiting. It's two o'clock in the morning. You know, you're a little under the weather, too." Be nice? Not ol' Charlie! Defiantly he orders, "Fill it up again," giving the bartender a bad time!

Finally, the bartender has all he can take, walks around the bar and grabs Charlie by the scruff of the neck. He yanks him off of the barstool, and drags ol' Charlie across the floor, and throws him onto the sidewalk! This example is a caricature of casting out a demon. They will not depart except by force.

A victim's problem will never be solved until that demon is extricated and his power broken. That is the biblical provision. You and I are the warriors to do that. Did you ever think of yourself that way, O mighty soldier of God?

If not, perhaps it is time to change your mind. No one else can change it for you. We are to pray always, but even more pointedly when Satan's minions softly but compellingly speak in our minds. That is the way he will approach. He is not going to say, "I'm the devil. Listen to me." He will say, "This is God speaking. Listen to me." Remember that he said, "I will be like the Most High" (Isaiah 14:14).

Or he will arrive with various expressions, pretending to be you. "I am you. These are your thoughts. They are not pleasant, but you're stuck with them because they're you. And how are you going to divide you from yourself? You can't do it. You're stuck with you."

But Hebrews 4:12 says that narrative is false! "For the word of God is quick, and powerful, and sharper than any two-edged sword, piercing even to the dividing asunder of soul and spirit, and of the joints and marrow, and is a discerner of the thoughts and intents of the heart." If we are to comprehend the separation of our soul from evil spirits who pretend to be "us", then it is the Word of God upon which we must feed ourselves. For it is the Word of the Lord who, on our behalf, will divide it for us. He separates our thoughts from the thoughts of the adversary. That is, the demons who constantly feed us every negative thing.

AUTHOR'S TESTIMONY

One time a crystal-clear word of the Lord was put into my mind. It came at a moment when I was wondering about a negative thought that had been interjected. While sitting in the Copper Skillet coffee shop in Kirkwood, Missouri in 1972, I was making notes on lovely things about my eight-year-old son. Pencil in hand, pondering what words I should write next, there it came.

All of the following took place within two seconds. Things of spirit do not require time because spirit is ever-present eternal; time being temporal. Many spiritual things can happen within one second of what we call time. This interchange took place in the spirit. It occurred as thought words without sound.

As I was looking up, suddenly a strongly negative thought crashed into my mind. And then on the other side of my mental screen came the Scripture, "...try the spirits whether they are of God" (I John 4:1). And so, I thought, "Are you of God?" He said, "No, you dumb [four dirty words]!!"

Wow! Wait a minute. Did this really happen? All of that was within a flash of time – it was swish, all that fast. Man, did that really happen? It was the most subtle thing that ever occurred to me in the realm of discerning of spirits. So, I went through it again. Here's what happened:

"As I'm sitting here, I'm making notes about my son, John. A thought came to me, and it didn't seem right; it was out of character. He is such a sweet son. On the back end of the loving thought, almost as though part of the original, the negative thought crashed in. Within the next split second the Lord prompted me to again challenge the negative thought-voice, which I did, "Are you of God?" Again, "No, you dumb [four dirty words]!!" Boom! In one second of time, there it was. The second challenge confirmed the first.

So, I flipped my pages over to start a fresh page of notes. Excited, I began to write words in praise to God. He fingered something new to me. How or why did it happen? Because I was meditating in the Word of God! Here were two opposing spirits speaking clear thought words from their respective places. The Lord says, "There are many kinds of voices in the world and none of them is without signification [significance]" (1 Corinthians 14:10). We are to decide which source we are going to tune in. Much as with television, a mental "clicker" is ours to control. We are to think upon that which is godly, pure, holy, just, righteous, virtuous, of good report (Philippians 4:8). If a thought does not measure up to that, shut it off. It does not belong in your mind.

Our heart is deceitful and desperately wicked says Jeremiah 17:9. Comparing it to a cabbage, when you see the outer leaf with a wormhole, naturally you peel it away. Doing so reveals the next two or three just like the first. How typical of deliverance. The obvious is ejected. Yet, amid the normal abrasions of life, other traits and behaviors cause us to evaluate further. "Is this also demonic, or is it merely the carnal nature on display?"

Let there be no misapprehensions. Both are real.

When you receive a deliverance, it is glorious and wonderful. It is movement in the right direction. You are reaching toward the "mark for the prize of the high calling of God in Christ Jesus" (Philippians 3:14). Yes. You are on the right course, but it is not over. You still have hope of entering into heaven, but you are not there yet.

It bears repeating that I have never cast only one evil spirit out of a needy person. Like roaches, where there is one, there are usually more. Their eggs that can still be hatched are the remaining elements of our old nature [see Galatians 5:19-20].

The question is asked, "Are all improper thoughts from a demon?" No. Our own heart is evil also. Negative thoughts arise from the lusts of our fallen nature. Apostle Paul explained that his battles were between the opposing natures within (See Romans 7:14-25). The Lord permitted a messenger of Satan [a demon] to buffet him in what Paul called his "thorn in the flesh" (See 2 Corinthians 12:7). He also said he often was unable to do the righteous things he wanted to do, being unable to stop doing unrighteous things which he did not want to do. He had constant warfare in his mind, just as we do (Romans 8:7). No believer among us is greater than Apostle Paul.

TESTIMONY OF A LADY AT SEMINAR

A woman came to our meeting in hope of finding help for her adult son. She believed her son was "demon-possessed". He had a high IQ and was living with a woman who was not his wife.

Appealing in distress, she said in distress, "I feel the Lord brought me here. There must be something I can do. My own son is demon-possessed, very brilliant, an intellectual. He found the Lord; he wrote an epic about the fight between good and evil; and it ends in the most triumphant way. He is called to be a genius and there has been a lot of interest in producing this epic as a stage production.

"It never seemed to convict his conscience that he was living in a way that did not glorify the Lord, but we kept on witnessing. One night at his girlfriend's house, he went completely berserk, literally out of his mind. I had never seen or heard anything like this before; it was completely beyond anything I could imagine. We were engulfed in a strange atmosphere. It wasn't my son anymore. He grabbed my wrist and blurted out, 'You know I love you! You know I love you! You know I love you!' Then suddenly, he blasphemed, frothed at the mouth, and spoke in some strange language. This went on for an hour and a half!

My husband and I both recognized that there was demon possession. I never had any experience in this, and my husband was rather far away from the Lord. I spoke as I had heard, to cast out demons. After about an hour and a half, he finally quieted down, looked up at me, smiled, and was himself again. He had gone completely out of his mind and doesn't remember it."

She added, "He was living with the wrong woman. I tell you one thing. This event broke up that relationship, but good! After that, there was an unnatural restlessness, talkativeness, and a manic kind of expression. It lasted through the duration of his automobile trip half-way across the country and back. Now he seems to be better, but I feel there is still some evil within him. It's not finished, and I need to know what to do about it. Like Mr. Pilcher, I'm a Missouri Synod Lutheran and there seems to be really no one in our church who understands these things."

I asked if her son was located near our city. She said, "No, he lives in New Jersey, separated from his wife, and living with another woman." Asked if her son was aware of his need, she replied, "He is very troubled inside. He doesn't fully accept that he could be demon-possessed. He went to a séance seeking wisdom. That must have been what triggered this."

In a situation like this, the entire family is in crisis, but most urgently the one in need of deliverance. The most important thing loved ones can do is to begin praying with other believers who believe in Christian deliverance ministry. Prayers must be fervent and not just token expressions. Serious matters need a serious response. Prayer warriors need to be willing to intercede until there is breakthrough. The victim must acknowledge his need and seek help for his own deliverance.

A friend of mine, Dan Malachuk - a seasoned deliverance minister and publisher of Logos Magazine - lived near this young man in Watchem, New Jersey. I offered to refer him to her son.

His mother asked, "Was it wrong for me to try to cast demons out of him?" I replied, "No! You were not wrong! You got results when you prayed! You did the absolute best thing for your son, but it is clear that more needs to be done."

We added her son's name to our prayer list, where it would remain until we heard news of his deliverance. When choices are limited, this is the expedient thing to do. Prayer is a powerful weapon against an entrenched enemy, and its effectiveness must not be minimized. Faith is good, and believing is good, but these are not prayer. Faithful believers must actually pray the words, in addition to professing faith and belief. God answers prayers that are prayed, not just spiritual belief.

A cogent example of this principle is seen in Jonah chapter 2:2-7. In the worst possible condition, dying in a great fish's belly, in blackness on the bottom of the sea, Jonah truly had desperation, faith and belief. But these did not rescue him. Finally, he screamed his prayers to God. It was only after he cried out that the Lord came to his rescue. That is our example to follow: when we fervently pray the words, God will answer. Fervent praying is the difficult work that must be done. Did Jonah's prayer have to be formal, or in special words, or even within the hearing or knowledge of another human? Did it even have to be intelligible to anyone else? Was there an altar at hand? Did he have to walk down an aisle in public? The answer to all these questions is a resounding "NO!" Like many others he was in an unspeakable, horrible prison, good as dead, without help or hope. Within moments he would have been dead unless he had prayed. From the Lord's perspective, this was the ideal circumstance. He looks for true sincerity, whether the person is kneeling at an altar or not. As Jonah prayed in desperation, "…the Lord spake unto the fish, and it vomited out Jonah upon the dry land" (Jonah 2:10).

God answers prayer, not belief without words. As to the final result of the lady's prayer request on behalf of her son, we never heard from her again. That is not unusual. We pray and leave the matter in the hands of the Lord. We are told in I Samuel 16:7, "…for the Lord seeth not as a man seeth; for man looketh on the outward appearance, but the Lord looketh upon the heart."

CHAPTER FOUR

THOUGHTS AND IMAGINATIONS

"It is impossible to divorce the mind from the body. If the mind is disturbed, the body will carry a hundred disturbances." – H.A. Maxwell Whyte

Observing the life of King David, we learn that yielding to temptation is never right. Moreover, when it arises out of the immodesty of a temptress, it may cause disastrous consequences. Both old and modern cultures have glorified nudity to the point of their ruination. The motive behind the exhibition of nakedness is to generate impure erotic thoughts. These are quickly magnified by eager agents of the devil, for whom our fallen nature is a fertile feeding ground. That is why Scripture admonishes believers to monitor and limit thought-voices to the standard set by the Holy Spirit, notably in Philippians 4:8 and Galatians 5:22-23. While that may first appear to be an easy thing to do, it is not, and for that reason most people make little effort to do so. Another reason is that many do not know that control of our thoughts is possible and have never even considered it.

The process of rejecting an impure thought is the same for all types of temptation. Mental violations of biblical principles include all manner of behaviors in personal relationships, negative attitudes, and private compulsions. God has written his standard for righteous thought and conduct. If there is mental confusion in how to deal with any moral subject, it can be clarified by reading the Bible's straightforward declarations. There are no secret codes or mysteries that require elaborate teaching or writing of extra-biblical books to clarify them.

Like other notables, such as Samson with Delilah and King Ahab with Jezebel, King David did not always check his thoughts before acting on them. Chosen of God, he is described as "…ruddy and of a beautiful countenance …". That means he was very handsome. Moreover, he was destined to replace Saul as King of Israel. To equip him for the assignment, the Spirit of the Lord came upon David, as revealed in I Samuel 16:14. Simultaneously, "The Spirit of the Lord departed from Saul [the king], and an evil spirit from the Lord troubled him." Notice that the evil spirit was from the Lord - stated five times for emphasis. Verses 15-18: "And Saul's servants said unto him, Behold now, an evil spirit from God troubleth thee. Let our lord now command thy servants, which are before thee, to seek out a man, who is a cunning player on an harp: and it shall come to pass, when the evil spirit from God is upon thee, that he shall play with his hand, and thou shalt be well. And Saul said unto his servants, provide me now a man that can play well, and bring him to me. Then answered one of the servants, and said, Behold, I have seen a son of Jesse the Bethlehemite, that is cunning in playing, and a mighty valiant man, and a man of war, and prudent in matters, and a comely person, and the Lord is with him." Who would imagine such a glowing commendation of a young sheep herder! David had such a reputation early in life.

First Samuel 16:19-23, "Wherefore Saul sent messengers unto Jesse, and said, send me David thy son, which is with the sheep. And Jesse took an ass laden with bread, and a bottle of wine, and a kid, and sent them by David his son to Saul. And David came to Saul and stood before him: and he [Saul] loved him greatly; and he became his armor-bearer. And Saul sent to Jesse, saying, Let David, I pray thee, stand before me; for he hath found favour in my sight. And it came to pass, when the evil spirit from God was upon Saul, that David took a harp, and played with his hand: so, Saul was refreshed, and was well, and the evil spirit departed from him." What a marvelous truth is seen in this Scripture! When evil spirits are vexing and harassing you, begin to play or sing godly music right where you are. If your singing sounds like an old crow, sing on. It is God who gave you that voice and he expects you to sing in thanksgiving and praise. Doing so will change your mood as well as the atmosphere, for the Lord so loves godly music that he leans in close to embrace your worship. That is when evil spirits flee! Along with singing, you should also command evil spirits to depart.

David's life was quite ordinary at first, but his innate talents and gift of music were so specially anointed that he was summoned by the Sovereign to play in the court of the king. He wrote glorious psalms under the anointing of the Holy Spirit, to be revered, sung, and prayed by all succeeding generations. Nearly every believer quotes and takes comfort from his magnificent Psalms 23, 91, 103 and so many others.

Second Samuel 5:4 says, "David was thirty years old when he began to reign, and he reigned for forty years." The characterization of him having laudable talents, special anointing, promoted from shepherd boy to King of a great nation, beloved of Israel, the "apple of God's eye", and loved by his nation, serves to highlight the enigma that was the life of this man. Important lessons for us are discovered in the narrative.

In 2 Samuel 11:2-5 we read: "And it came to pass in an evening tide, that David arose from off his bed, and walked upon the roof of the king's house: and from the roof he saw a woman washing herself; and the woman was very beautiful to look upon ..." There is nothing wrong with a woman being very beautiful, since beauty has not been earned but is a divine gift to be safeguarded in modesty. There is nothing wrong with a king walking on the roof of his house. And though a little quirky, there also may be no ordinance against a beautiful woman washing herself where she – either by chance or on purpose, would be seen, and a man, by chance, seeing her. He might smile and think of it as a delightful happenstance ... quickly turn his head again to confirm the vision he thought he saw, then look a bit more. It surely happened with him that evening, just as it does with men and women everywhere, even when the attraction is less alluring than beautiful Bathsheba in her bubble bath. The sight of an innocent, beautiful person is a blessing to every honorable viewer. The question becomes, what happens next? Let us enter into a possible and somewhat facetious thought process that might have occurred.

Headline: Righteous King sees naked

lady: "Whoa!" Suddenly the serene majesty of 'righteousness, peace, and joy in the Holy Ghost' is in shock mode:

"All you majestic thoughts – hold up a moment, while I scout out this intrusion. I must examine it to see whether national security is threatened.

Hmmmm. Or could the Lord be giving me a new inspiration?

(Psalm 92:8, "For thou, Lord, hast made me glad through thy work.")

"Hmmmm. I could always use another secretary. An interview couldn't hurt anything."

"Oh, Butler, call two messengers."

On this occasion, "… David sent and inquired after the woman. And one said, Is not this Bathsheba, the daughter of Eliam, the wife of Uriah the Hittite?" First, the servants were sent to "inquire". Next, "And David sent messengers, and took her; and she came in unto him, and he lay with her; for she was purified from her uncleanness: and she returned unto her house. And the woman conceived, and sent and told David, and said, I am with child." It is astonishing how much the Lord packs into four words! These alone could make a two-hour movie! Do you remember Jesus talking about "… the beginning of sorrows"? With this report, David suddenly saw it unfolding before his eyes!

For context, let us rehearse the reputation,

character, achievements, and apparent nature of the man. Here was David, the nation's king, anointed of the Lord, handsome, strong, courageous, a true warrior who led Israel's armies to great victories, single-handedly killing a bear and a lion to rescue a lamb!

(First Samuel 17:34-35 and 49-51) He killed a 12-foot-tall giant by slinging a single stone into his forehead and chopping off his head with the giant's own sword. He was bright and prudent in matters, loved by all the people. Surely his life seemed utopian.

Now place your judgment into this situation. The King was up for a night walk on the roof of his palace to consider weighty matters of state - the raging battle of his army against Amorite hordes, the blessing of his godly family and wealth - just to think a little while. Great leaders do this. Why else would he take a night walk by himself? It would have been a quiet time of fellowship with God in the cool of the evening. In peace and solitude, he would look into the heavens glowing with billions of stars and be inspired to compose yet another psalm to glorify God. If you were a righteous King as gifted as he, isn't that what you would be doing?

In that exalted frame of mind, his eye catches a glimpse of a "very beautiful" naked lady washing herself. Remember, David already had at least seven beautiful wives who could satisfy any possible desire he might imagine in the comforts of bed, bath, or playtime. Right here something happened, but what was it?

Let us now examine a fact of his circumstance, which also has relevance to us. What do you do when naked beauty registers in your mind? (In a live seminar, the only response to this question was laughter from the audience! That tells us something.) Scripture makes a point of emphasizing Bathsheba's beauty. She was a knock-out, strikingly beautiful – fit for a king. A thought enters. This is the critical moment for any man or woman. What do you do when a provocative thought is subtly interjected into your mind? Before an impure motive could have developed, David could have and should have averted his eyes and purposely envisioned the beauty of his own wives. They also took luxurious baths and sprayed a hint of the King's favorite perfume to create an intoxicating effect. He made sure they were beautiful at the outset and that they remained so. In this instance, he could have switched his mind to challenge any questionable thought and ask himself the critical question:

Is this thought true, virtuous, pure, just, holy, of good report? Is this a thought from God? (See the Lord's requirement at Philippians 4:8). We may surmise that David did not challenge his thoughts by that standard on this evening. Between the first time he saw, thought about, and enquired of her, to the time he actually sent for her, he had done a lot of thinking. Impure thoughts had found their way in and progressed to an evil motive. He sent at least two messengers to her with an appeal that pleased her. She gladly accompanied the next pair of messengers into the King's magnificent palace. The Bible wastes no time or words in explaining what happened (2 Samuel 11:5): David and Bathsheba had a devilish affair in the king's palace, and she got pregnant.

Clearly David was guilty. But what about Bathsheba? Was her conduct righteous and pure? It was known to those serving in the palace, that she was married to the king's warrior, Uriah. Pages 34 and 128 of Ungers Bible Dictionary denote that Bathseba's grandfather, Ahithophel, was a highly esteemed advisor to David in the king's court, with access to privileged information. Lonesome at home, while her valiant husband was deployed in far off military battles, she well knew he might be killed, never to return. This is the usual mind set of soldiers' wives who await their husband's return from long periods of deployment. That fear almost immediately became fact, for he was indeed killed.

The rich, handsome king was adored by his people. Bathsheba was still beautiful, perhaps thinking they might be "a match" together. This thought also quickly became the fact. Objectively, it would appear that bathing in open view seems less like modesty and more like a set-up with an ulterior motive. She was not raped but consented to visit privately with David in his bedroom. Another fact of Scripture is that when any type of lust is conceived, its voracious appetite can never be satisfied; it can only be fed. James 1:15 explains: "Then when lust hath conceived, it bringeth forth sin; and sin, when it is finished, bringeth forth death."

When Bathsheba sent word that she was with child, what did David do? Second Samuel 11:6-11 tells us, "... David sent to Joab [general of the army] saying, Send me the soldier, Uriah the Hittite [husband of Bathsheba]. And Joab sent Uriah to David. And when Uriah was come unto him, David demanded of him [in evasive cheap talk] how Joab did, and how the people did, and how the war prospered. And David said to Uriah, Go down to thy house, and wash thy feet. And Uriah departed out of the king's house, and there followed him a mess of meat from the king. But Uriah slept at the door of the king's house with all the servants of his lord and went not down to his house. And when they had told David, saying, Uriah went not down unto his house, David said unto Uriah, [in more evasive cheap talk] camest thou not from thy journey? Why then didst thou not go down unto thine house? And Uriah said unto David, the Ark, and Israel, and Judah, abide in tents; and my lord Joab, and the servants of my lord, are encamped in the open fields; shall I then go into mine house, to eat and to drink, and lie with my wife? as thou livest, and as thy soul liveth, I will not do this thing."

David was stuck with a loyal, impeccably honorable soldier on his hands, a guy who had genuine camaraderie with his buddies in battle. Uriah was not looking for special favors and privileges from the king. He would reject all such offers of privilege. David's scheme had been to bring Uriah in from the battlefield and grant him bedroom "rest and relaxation" with his wife. The king even sent meat! If his scheme had worked, he would have complimented Uriah in feigned innocence: "Congratulations. Advisors tell me you and your wife are going to have a child!"

But Uriah, uncommonly valorous, in empathy with soldier buddies and loyalty to his king, did not go to see his wife. What a shocking disappointment this had to be to David. The King had been caught in his own trap. David would now try to solve his problem the only way he knew. Hiding his own sin, he would send Uriah to the most intense front-line battle against overwhelming hordes of Amorites, where he would surely be killed. Redeployed against impossible odds, Uriah bravely fought and died on the battlefield – a hero murdered. When the report of his death came back, David, with a sigh of relief was able to take Uriah's suddenly widowed Bathsheba into his own house to become his wife – a murderous whoredom of the worst kind. If the King thought he was thereby free of the problem, he was wrong. That was not the end of the matter. His multiple sins demanded a horrific price to be paid. As sovereign and King he was free from human judgment but was not to escape the penalty for his crime. That's the way it always is. "God is not mocked!"

Second Samuel 12:1-7 tells us that God sent the Prophet Nathan to tell the king a story about a rich man taking advantage of a poor man. Feigning innocence and indignation, David says, "As the Lord liveth, the man that hath done this thing shall surely die!" As the oracle of God, Nathan turns to David and says, "Thou art the man!" Nathan knew it was mortally dangerous to challenge or insult a king, whose word is law. Other kings had killed prophets for less. But David's wise choice was to humble himself and confess. Nevertheless, while his own life would be spared, the penalty would be swift in coming. We learn from this that many sins, though forgiven, still carry a penalty, which must be paid by the sinner.

Second Samuel 12:13-14 tells us, "And David said unto Nathan, I have sinned against the Lord. [Here he did not confess that his sin was also against Uriah whom he murdered. Still, all sins against a human are also sins against God]. And Nathan said unto David, The Lord also hath put away thy sin; thou shalt not die. Howbeit, because by this deed thou hast given great occasion to the enemies of the

Lord to blaspheme, the child also that is born unto thee shall surely die. And Nathan departed unto his house. And the Lord struck the child that Uriah's wife bare unto David, and it was very sick." David pleaded with the Lord in fasting for a week to heal his son, but the child died. This was only the first of even more disastrous punishment to come. The sin David committed was heinous, indeed. We are still reading about it 2700 years after the fact. Yet, remarkably, when the same sin of adultery is committed by a modern televangelist, it is vastly more destructive to the Kingdom of God than was the fall of David. Its publicity gives instant worldwide "occasion to the enemies of the Lord to blaspheme". Knowing this should seriously humble offenders and render them repentant and meek, rather than dismissive of their crime and boastful of their imprisonment for it, as though they had been unjustly penalized.

The next immediate consequence of David's sin was the beginning of plagues upon the land of Israel. If only he had challenged that lustful thought the moment it entered his mind, he could have defeated it. Imagine the agonies that would have been avoided had he done so. We are not different 27 centuries later. God warned us of sin's punishment: (Numbers 32:23b) "... be sure, your sin will find you out." When we let an unholy thought ferment to the point of an evil imagination, it leads to a fantasy, and the fantasy evolves into a plan, which is then executed. It is possible and scripturally enjoined that we interrupt and challenge every thought, either to cease, or bend to compliance with the Philippians 4:8 standard of purity.

David did not do that, but you and I can. David's unchallenged chain of thoughts wreaked havoc on his own family and his entire nation. His baby died, his wives were carried away captive, plagues were sent to destroy thousands of civilians, and more thousands of David's soldiers were killed by enemies sent by the Lord. This tremendous destruction was the direct result of his failure to comply before his thought became unstoppable. Instead, he allowed it to take him into sin. We must recognize that our fallen nature is in collusion with evil spirits who are provocateurs, ever speaking evil thoughts into our mind. We have both the power and responsibility to challenge them. Second Corinthians 10:5 instructs us: "Casting down imaginations, and every high thing that exalteth itself against the knowledge of God and bringing into captivity every thought to the obedience of Christ."

This nexus of disobedience and punishment is perennial. In Noah's day the Lord was profoundly angered, seeing that (Genesis 6:5-7) "… every imagination of the thoughts of [man's] heart was only evil continually", and because of it He determined, "I will destroy man from the face of the earth; both man, and beast…for it repenteth me that I have made them." Thus, He did so, saving only Noah and his family during the flood-water judgment. The only difference between the thoughts of David and those of the Genesis 6 population is how widespread the problem had become. Nobody ever "gets away with" anything in the end because every thought, motive, word, and deed is recorded for playback on the day the Lord judges each of us face to face.

David's own writing shows what he knew: "... goodness and mercy shall follow me all the days of my life: and I will dwell in the house of the Lord forever" (Psalm 23:6). But his experience at this time was not at that high point. Rather, it was his time of shame, loss, guilt, and mourning. He would have recalled reading about Job's loss and calamity – losing his entire family, health, and wealth. Even his wife mocked him, saying, "Why don't you curse God and die?" Of course, she, too, was suffering the great loss, except that her health had not been taken, as was her husband's.

Again, what about Bathsheba? Her mind would be rehearsing how all this came about – the guilt of adultery, David's murder of her husband Uriah, the dispiriting whisper campaign, and sorrow at the death of her child. Her earlier hope of a good and plenteous life with the handsome king, having unlimited servants and maids in the palace, enjoying prestige among the people, her nine months of pregnancy in hopeful expectancy - all were tarnished and in vain. Her child was dead. She, too, mourned the disappointment and loss. The guilt and shame of her morose husband was also to be hers. The marriage had been legal, all right, but it was unrighteous and sinful. All her joyous dreams were shattered under the law: "Be not deceived; God is not mocked: for whatsoever a man soweth, that shall he also reap" (Galatians 6:7). In marriage, what affects one partner equally affects the spouse and family. Worse, when the marriage is of the King and Queen, the whole nation must also pay a price for their sins.

In Matthew 5:28 Jesus warns, "But I say unto you, that whosoever looketh on a woman to lust after her hath committed adultery with her already in his heart." This applies equally to men and women. It is clear that the Lord sees our motive. Lust had not been conceived in David's heart the first instant he saw Bathsheba naked. His pulse might have jumped for a second or two, and he might have turned his head twice and smiled – just to confirm the vision. It is unclear whether Bathsheba had planned intentionally to attract the king's attention, but room is left for suspicion. She knew that nudity is one thing that always attracts attention. So do the ladies of today.

Many Scripture verses speak of lust. Two of them are: James 1:14-15 and 1 John 2:16. "But every man is tempted, when he is drawn away of his own lust, and enticed. Then when lust hath conceived, it bringeth forth sin; and sin, when it is finished, bringeth forth death." That truth is forcefully seen in David and Bathsheba's affair. The second verse is: "For all that is in the world, the lust of the flesh, and the lust of the eyes, and the pride of life, is not of the Father, but is of the world." We see that lust pervades the world in all its evil dimensions – evil because lust is opposite to righteousness and holiness.

Lust developed in David's heart at some point between his first sight of naked Bathsheba and the time they interviewed in his palace. Consummation of his lustful arousal was not long in coming. Not to dwell on that point, our study is mainly of thoughts that precede the development of an imagination before it progresses to an impure fantasy that culminates in a sinful act. Every normal, healthy husband often notices an attractive lady in public, usually clothed in accordance with protocol. It is more pronounced when exhibition is immodest and provocative. Ladies are aware of this "quirk" in men, and many revel in it to excess - a pathetic "look at me" ploy.

In the divine context, the lust problem of David and Bathsheba was exposed for the ultimate benefit of themselves, and for all successive generations who would learn of it. What ultimately came out of it was the maturing of the greatest King of the most important nation ever in the world. He was to rule from Jerusalem, Israel, God's chosen land, people, and ultimately to be the Lord's world headquarters. The outworking of their torrid affair and God's judgments upon their sins, was that their troubled marriage produced the wisest man who ever lived on earth, King Solomon, who wrote three of the Holy Bible's 66 books. Their content is fitting in that their subjects are love, wisdom, and vanity. All succeeding generations of believers have studied and depended upon the marvelous truths contained in Song of Solomon, The Proverbs, and Ecclesiastes. In them we learn that kings and clerics alike think and do wrongly, as we all do, only to pay a heavy price for moral failures.

> *Courage, strength, and fearlessness are no match for the raw power of lustful thoughts.*

From the Lord's point of view, it was necessary to give us the example of David and Bathsheba. Isaiah 1:18 speaks of forgiveness: "Though your sins be as scarlet they shall be white as snow." This truth is reflected in the forgiveness and honor granted to David. God Himself, in human flesh as the Lord Jesus Christ, made it known to the whole world for all time that He was to be identified as "the Son of David". The very first verse of the first Gospel – penned by Matthew, declares: "The book of the generation of Jesus Christ, the son of David..." Though Jesus' sufferings for our sin were far more intense than

David's was for his sin, both had experienced the deadly price to be paid for sin, and both were highly exalted after humbling themselves. We are thus assured that our sins, likewise, will be forgiven after confessing and turning away from them, and we also shall be exalted. We are forgiven when we "stop doing it", not before, whether they be actions or attitudes. In Psalm 32:5 David acknowledged his sin, the sorrow it brought, and the Lord's mercy in forgiving him.

MEETING THE CONDITIONS FOR DELIVERANCE

The more I have worked in the deliverance ministry, the more I have seen its ongoing need. Just because a person receives a genuine deliverance one time, does not necessarily mean it was the only deliverance that was needed. The first evil spirit that enters into your life - thereby becoming the "strong man" - usually will be the last to go out. Demons do not die when expelled but live to counterattack over our lifetime. Christians should never be embarrassed to admit we need help! The devil's forces are cunning and relentless, requiring us to take both defensive and offensive action. I personally examine my life carefully to find and challenge any aberrant motive, thought, malady, or behavior that needs to be amended.

While I have wanted to move off this subject – as so many others have done – the Lord has seen fit to keep me focused on deliverance, in both the broad and narrow sense. If the church body does not learn of this type of spiritual warfare she shall remain in ignorance to her further detriment, only to needlessly suffer avoidable torments. Generally, the church body is not sophisticated in knowledge of our adversary. It is my hope that you will embrace and relay this more detailed message to someone else, that it may eventually penetrate throughout the Church. Telling others is our task. Friend and former pastor associate, Rev. Rodney G. Lynch, was concerned that we not just preach on elimination of the negative. I am concerned about that too. We know there is no deliverance outside of Jesus Christ the Lord, and He must be our emphasis. Yet, you cannot fully put on the new man Christ Jesus, without putting off the old in direct proportion. The old man, mortally wounded by Christ, is officially and technically dead. We are to put him off, as we would discard the clothes of a stinking corpse. We initially put on the new man upon our new birth ["ye must be born again" John 3:7]. However, we continue to become Christianized - more like Jesus Christ - day by day. Putting off the old and putting on the new is a continuous process until death, and with each deliverance we become a purer image of the Son of God. When anyone preaches deliverance, he is preaching Jesus Christ! For He is the only Deliverer. While the word deliverance is somewhat general, here it is more specially applied to the evicting of evil spirits. But deliverance is more than that - eviction being one aspect. Notice that the words salvation and deliverance are used interchangeably:

In Joel 2:32: "And it shall come to pass, that whosoever shall call on the name of the Lord shall be delivered ..." and in Acts 2:21 Apostle Peter exactly quoted Joel 2:32 but used the word 'saved' in place of Joel's use of the word 'delivered'. Salvation is the first and primary deliverance, to be followed by lesser deliverances during faithful Christian service throughout one's lifetime. The primary requirement for receiving deliverance is to submit your life to the Lordship of Jesus Christ. That simply means to confess that you are a sinner in need of forgiveness and to ask Jesus Christ to forgive you. Turn from your evil ways and ask that He deliver you from sin and demons, then stay on that course.

BOOK OF THE LAW

Throughout this section, our reference to LAW excludes the ordinances that required Jews to make blood sacrifices and observe other rituals to cover their sins. Jesus fulfilled all of these in becoming the final Sacrifice for sin.

Sin is illegal in heaven and on earth. That is the law of God. What comprises sin is described throughout the Scripture narratives and word lists, among which are those in Galatians 5:19-21. Punishment for any one of them is eternal death.

Adam committed only one sin and was sentenced to death. Lucifer in heaven likewise sinned and was sentenced to death.

At the earth level of governance, men also make laws, violation of which brings punishment, including death. Though fully informed of this fact, man willfully violates all the laws of God and man. Law itself is good, of God, and remains in effect. Satan is the "lawless" one. Notice that the Holy Bible does not call itself the Book of Grace, or Book of Love, or Book of Mercy, or Book of Truth. While these are divine descriptions indeed, the Lord defines it as it The Book of the Law (Deuteronomy 31:26). It is the whole counsel of God for mankind, comprised of both Old and New Testaments. All intelligent beings, visible or invisible, are governed by its provisions. Psalm 119:89 tells us, "Forever, O Lord, thy word is settled in heaven." All other books fall within the purview of the Old and New Testaments.

There has already been enough interpretive quarreling over the relationship between biblical law and divine grace. Thus, this volume does not elaborate on it, as both remain valid. Meanwhile, let us consider one of the Ten Commandments: "Thou shalt not kill [literally, "do no murders"]. That commandment is part of the Book of the Law. We know that if this one provision alone is violated, the law is swift to incarcerate or kill the perpetrator. Law has not been repealed.

A further observation is that, while theologians haggle to justify conflicting views on grace versus law, it is wiser to view the matter from God's perspective.

1. He is the God, not only of time, but also of eternity. The Spirit replaces the Letter of the Law (2 Corinthians 3:6).
2. He declares "I change not." – "I am the same yesterday, today and forever." Time and its humanity are as a tiny bubble floating on the sea of eternity.

A human being is as a grain of sand among the trillions found on the world's seashores, or as a barely visible star in the universe of trillions. Most humans will never see heaven, because while "many are called, few are chosen" (Matthew 22:14), and God alone does the choosing (John 15:16).

Of all the declarations concerning grace and law, the over-riding, all-embracing command is "Thou shalt love the Lord thy God with all thy heart, all thy soul, all thy mind, and all thy strength, and thy neighbor as thyself."

Contained within these words are all the law and the prophets (Combining Matthew 22:37-40 with Luke 10:27). Anyone, anywhere who has never heard of Jesus or the law yet obeys this command by natural understanding within his culture, shall enter into heaven. Contrariwise, learned Pharisees and Bible scholars who disobey this command are in danger of hell fire (See John 8:23-24; John 10:16; and Romans 2:13-16).

How do you receive deliverance from evil spirits? The proven way is to learn the requirements of Scripture and obey them. God's laws and principles are available to guide all willful humans into all truth. We exercise our will to live either on the right side or on the wrong side of them. Our parents – Adam and Eve – had blessing when they were obedient, and curse when they disobeyed. That set the pattern for all of us. There is irony in the fact that a person can experience both at the same time. To wit: a man may be blessed with wealth, while suffering the curse of terminal cancer.

The detailed cases presented in this book will enlighten you in how to receive deliverance. You will probably see some of your own problems among them.

CANAAN & GIANTS = SALVATION & DEMONS

The Old Testament land of Canaan for Israel is a forward-looking picture of Salvation in the New Testament. Literal Canaan equals spiritual salvation. The hybrid giants - evil occupants of Canaan - represent evil spirits of the New Testament. Exodus

23:27-30 says, "I will send my fear before thee, and will destroy all the people to whom thou shalt come [Canaan's heathen kings and peoples], and I will make all thine enemies turn their backs unto thee. And I will send hornets before thee, which shall drive out the Hivite, the Canaanite, and the Hittite [types of demons], from before thee. I will not drive them out from before thee in one year; lest the land become desolate, and the beast of the field multiply against thee. By little and little I will drive them out from before thee, until thou be increased, and inherit the land."

On August 18, 1971, in attendance at a Kansas City convention, I was alone in my room having serious demonic intrusions. Having done all I knew to obtain release, and in desperation, I reached for my Bible and appealed, "God, show me something; I need some kind of relief!" This is exactly the verse my eyes fell upon: [Exodus 23:29]. It came as revelation that deliverance is not a onetime event but is progressive. You cannot have a truly major deliverance and instantly assimilate a new walk of life as though demons had not affected you. One woman had 70 evil spirits driven out in one night, but she could not perfectly maintain it. Seven years later, my wife and I again ministered deliverance to that dedicated Christian lady. Some of the same spirits who had been evicted the first time, had to be cast out the second time, along with others. I do not know anyone who was immediately able to walk in perfect righteousness without a period of assimilation after a deliverance of that magnitude. Her deliverance was a training ground for me. Do not insist that all the borders of your personal Canaan land have been secured. More than likely there are other giants to be defeated. It has been that way in my life and in others as well. That is nothing to be ashamed of, for this is "the normal Christian life". Rather, rejoice in each new freedom that is experienced.

Do not be anxious to be set free all at once. If God were to drive all evils out of you in one day, you wouldn't be able to handle it. Moreover, it is one thing to receive deliverance, quite another to keep it. As for me, I prefer to have one spirit permanently defeated and allow six months to assimilate the new freedom that should last forever.

An extension of the Exodus 23 message is seen in Deuteronomy 7:20-24. Psalm 149:7-9 shows that to bind wicked (spiritual) kings and nobles is a privilege granted to every believer in Christ: "… this honor have all his saints", working together with Christ.

FALSE GODS

Let us examine two additional verses that are pertinent here. Referencing the heathen inhabitants in Canaan: "The graven images of their gods shall ye burn with fire." What gods? False gods which are crafted, visible images of invisible demons. Deuteronomy 7:25-26 warns, "Thou shalt not desire the silver or gold that is on them, nor take it unto thee, lest thou be snared therein: for it is an abomination to the Lord thy God. Neither shalt thou bring an abomination into thine house, lest thou be a cursed thing like it: but thou shalt utterly detest it, and thou shalt utterly abhor it; for it is a cursed thing".

The warning is that if you have images or idols of false gods in your home, please get them out of your house! Troublesome demons attach to their dumb idols and images. Wherever you have their banners lifted up, the demons go with them. That includes images, idols, carvings, wall ornaments, paintings, or literature of a false god. (See the two cases of deliverance which illustrate the point in chapter two: The Ebony Mask, and David of Violence.

My wife and I prayed for Christians who had brought false gods into their homes. As we commanded them to depart, the bragging demons emphatically told us they did not have to depart. When demons say they don't have to leave, I stop and say, "Let's do a search of the house. There is something wrong here." In chapter two [Case of the Ebony Mask] a graven image was discovered in the house. As the image was being taken out, the demon yelled, "No, no, NO!" The moment the image was removed from the house, the demon screamed throughout his departure. The woman had hung an evil-laden, carved wood face on her bedroom wall. This is a typical scenario. Please understand that God magnifies his Word, the Book of the Law, above his holy name. It is not to be violated.

This means we should not sell or give them away even if valuable in money; for their demons would thereby be transferred to someone else. Break or burn them. Render them useless. Money is not the issue here. Several folks have balked in horror saying, "That's an expensive item! Do you know how much I paid for that?!" Well, what is it worth to you to have freedom from demons and the chaos they cause? There usually comes a time when a demon-oppressed individual will become so utterly desperate, he will do anything to be rid of the torment. If money is the difference between peace or torment, make your choice!

A woman in Alton, Illinois made an urgent call asking for personal ministry. I explained that we were in the process of moving to a new residence, while also preparing to teach a seminar on this subject and did not immediately have time to see her privately. I invited her to the seminar scheduled for Thursday, close to her home, where we would pray for her. Her response? "I'm busy on Thursday." Irritated by her selfishness, I said, "So am I." She asked if there was someone else she could go to. I turned her over to my wife, Nancy, to talk for a while. The response from that woman turned me off. Listen, when you have been at the gates of hell, and it is taking Jesus Christ the Lord to bring you out of it, I weary of people saying, "I'm too busy." Such folks are always welcome to go to somebody else – if another can be found to provide "miracles on demand". When you're desperate, you will seek deliverance at any price! If you play around and let card games and other things displace an appointment with the Lord, do not suppose that you will receive deliverance. Repentance is required first.

We present the Book of the Law, which is the Word of God. Some ask, "Well, Dave, look, aren't you talking about the Old Testament? Aren't we on grace? Why are you talking about the law?" The Scripture replies, "I came not to do away with the law, but to fulfill it" (Matthew 5:17-18). After all, it was pre-incarnate Jesus who gave the law in the first place. He says through Malachi 3:6a: "For I am the Lord, I change not;" Furthermore, in the New Testament we are informed, "All the promises of God are in him, yea and amen" (2 Corinthians 1:20). Most promises are legally qualified, having conditions that must be met before they can be fulfilled.

Consider that death itself is part of the body of law. Everybody must die, only because we have obeyed "the law of sin and death" in violation of "the law of the Spirit of life". "If ye live after the flesh, ye shall die but if ye through the Spirit do mortify [put off] the deeds of the body, ye shall live. In other words, obey the law (Romans 8:1-13). Under the best of conditions our body still has to die because it participated in sins of the flesh. "Verily, every man at his best state is altogether vanity" (Psalm 39:5).

Deuteronomy 30:10-20 says in part, "...harken unto the voice of the Lord thy God, to keep his commandments and his statutes which are written in this book of the law, and...turn unto the Lord thy God with all thine heart, and with all thy soul. For this commandment which I command thee this day, it is not hidden from thee, neither is it far off. It is not in heaven, that thou shouldest say, Who shall go up for us to heaven, and bring it unto us, that we may hear it, and do it? Neither is it beyond the sea, that thou shouldest say, Who shall go over the sea for us, and bring it unto us, that we may hear it, and do it? But the word is very nigh unto thee, in thy mouth, and in thy heart, that thou mayest do it. See, I have set before thee this day life and good, and death and evil."

In Joshua 1:8 the Lord said, "This book of the law shall not depart out of thy mouth; but thou shalt meditate therein day and night, that thou mayest observe to do according to all that is written therein: for then thou shalt make thy way prosperous, and then thou shalt have good success."

Psalms 1:1-3: "Blessed is the man whose delight is in the law of the Lord. In his law doth he meditate day and night. Whatsoever he doeth shall prosper."

Matthew 5:18: "For verily I say unto you, till heaven and earth pass, one jot or one tittle shall in no wise pass from the law, till all be fulfilled."

Hebrews 8:10, "...I will put my laws in their mind, and write them in their hearts..."

Hebrews 10:16, "...I will put my laws into their hearts, and in their minds will I write them."

James 2:8-11 "If ye fulfil the royal law according to the Scripture, Thou shalt love thy neighbor as thyself, ye do well. But if ye have respect to persons, ye commit sin, and are convinced of the law as transgressors. For whosoever shall keep the whole law, and yet offend in one point, he is guilty of all." God uses the same words many times. These are the God-given laws that govern what happens in your life. If you obey, you receive blessing. If you disobey, cursing.

All visible and invisible "persons" are unavoidably governed by God's law. Each of us decides to live on one side or the other. Satan is called prince of this world in John 14:30, and the god of this world in 2 Corinthians 4:4. If humans were to be rescued from the death penalty for violating the Law, an innocent life must be sacrificed in place of the guilty. God had told Adam in words similar to these: "The day you disobey me you will surely die." Death was the penalty for disobeying the words of God; God's Word is law.

Do you know the whole Bible? Do you know all the law? No, not by memory. Yet its principles are written in our heart. Can you be penalized for breaking a law that you do not know? Yes. Did you ever get a traffic ticket for speeding? If you say, "Yes officer, I was going 50 miles an hour in a residential area, but I didn't know what the speed limit was. I didn't see a sign." Are you excused because you did not know? No. He gives you a citation for dangerously violating the speed laws. The traffic court judge listens to your sad story, and, whether you knew the law or not, says, "The information has long been available to you. Now pay your fine."

Is that fair or unfair when it comes to God's law? If you do not know the law of God and violate its provisions, does the principal change? With or without our intellectual or "head knowledge" the Holy Spirit guides us into all truth (Psalms 31:3, and John 16:13). In the model prayer often called "the Lord's Prayer", Jesus illustrates by reciting: "Thy will be done on earth as it is in heaven." Here we see that earthlings operate under the heavenly system of law that demands obedience. A law that is broken automatically activates its punitive provisions. This refers to thoughts and conduct that are under our direct control, not to our primary salvation which is beyond human attainment. If you are born again, the call to repent was initiated by the Lord: "Ye have not chosen me, but I have chosen you…" (John 15:16).

Most often, Christians experience evil spirit problems because they have violated what God warned us not to do. Excuses are varied: "Well, I was only kidding, I was only teasing. We were just playing around! I didn't know about Ouija boards and fortune tellers! We only did it for fun and games." Not in God's eyes.

God says do not do it. It is an abomination. It is you who gives legal right and advantage to the devil, whether you know it or not! It is not a matter of what you know, or what you think, or what you choose to believe. Just as the judge in traffic court says, the information is available to us, we are responsible to know. If we choose not to know, the penalty falls upon us. The Bible, in its many translations, makes it abundantly clear what God's laws are, what his desire is for us. Some of the penalties are defined, but many are not – such as self-induced diseases through rebellious conduct. We must avail ourselves of the readily available knowledge or suffer a penalty for disobedience. Scripture shows that ignorance does not fully excuse us.

Leviticus 5:17-19 says, "...if a soul sin, and commit any of these things which are forbidden to be done by the commandments of the Lord; though he wist [knew] it not, yet is he guilty, and shall bear his iniquity. And he shall bring a ram without blemish out of the flock, with thy estimation, for a trespass offering, he hath certainly trespassed against the Lord." A blood sacrifice must be made to atone for sin. In Luke 12:48, the Lord provides another example. While a sin's penalty must be paid, it will be less if the offender does not know. "But he that knew not, and did commit things worthy of stripes, shall be beaten with few stripes. For unto whomsoever much is given, of him shall be much required: and to whom men have committed much, of him they will ask the more." He that knows and violates the law will be beaten with many stripes. He that does not know the law and violates it, will still be beaten, but with fewer stripes than were earned by an outright rebel.

Acts 3:17-19, "And now, brethren, I wot [know] that through ignorance ye did it [sinned], as did also your rulers. But those things, which God before had shewed by the mouth of all his prophets, that Christ should suffer, he hath so fulfilled. Repent ye therefore, and be converted, that your sins may be blotted out, when the times of refreshing shall come from the presence of the Lord." Repent, that your sins may be blotted out. They are still called sins whether you are knowledgeable or ignorant.

We saw in Deuteronomy that having a graven image in your house is an abomination to the Lord. An abomination is something that is detestable or hateful to God. Every place where abominations occur there is demonic activity. The very first words the Lord said to man by way of commandment was,

"Thou shalt have no other gods before me." No directive could be more emphatic. False gods are demons. Their ploy is to intrigue humans to make idols "in their demonic image" for believers to bring into their homes and lives. It would be difficult to overemphasize the importance of that fact. Understanding it will shield against wrong thinking and its negative consequences. False religions are replete with millions of images of demon gods, most notably in India, Asia, and parts of Europe.

It may seem offensive to a believer in Jesus Christ to point out that no one knows what Jesus looks like, apart from Isaiah explaining in general that he was not handsome. Isaiah 53:2b states: "…he hath no form nor comeliness; and when we shall see him, there is no beauty that we should desire him." What could be plainer than that? He was a "plain-looking" man. Yet, sincere believers hang on the walls of their homes, chapels, and cathedrals billions of painted and sculpted images created in artisans' imaginations - many of them beautiful to behold, but hardly Jewish in appearance - if there is such a thing - all the while knowing that Jesus was 100% Jew. Why is that? Images are false portrayals of the Invisible God, who purposely left no images of Himself to be worshiped or adored: "The just shall live by faith" (Romans 1:17), not by sight!

Whether images are little or large makes no moral difference! It also matters little whether you worship it. Even neck chains and molded images of so-called Saint Christopher, et al, are the equivalent of rubbing a rabbit's foot to bring good luck. Do not in any way or degree depend upon something or someone instead of Jesus Christ. Anyone or anything that has ever been worshiped as a god, is tantamount to a graven image and a sin for you to bring it into your home. If that statement seems radical, the point may be argued with the Divine Author of the Scriptures. Anytime you have doubt about an image, regardless of its form - carved, painted, molded, a stack of stones, an evergreen tree, or an apparition, give God the benefit of the doubt and get it out of house and possession for your own sake. "For there is one God, and one mediator between God and men, the man Christ Jesus" according to I Timothy 2:5, and he remains invisible. Again, as far as images go, if in doubt, throw them out!

Pray the marvelous prayer that King David prayed in Psalms 31:9: "Have mercy upon me, O Lord, for I am in trouble"! How utterly true and simple and profound that prayer is for each of us to pray! Amen.

CHAPTER FIVE

ANGELS AND DEMONS IN HUMAN AFFAIRS

THOUGHTS, IMAGINATIONS, VOICES,
DREAMS, VISIONS, INTERVENTIONS

The Holy Bible does not exist apart from its disclosure of the invisible, supernatural beings who have dwelt among us from our beginning. Had it not been so, the Lord would not have taught us to pray as in Luke 11:4: "... and deliver us from evil [literally, "the evil one"]. It is because they live among, on, and oftentimes inside us that we are instructed to pray that prayer. We are to become aware of their existence, the role they play in our individual lives, and in the governments of all nations. We are wise to acknowledge that Satan is god of this world and prince of this world, - not just of your nation (see 2 Corinthians 4:4 and John 14:30).

DOES EVIL ACTUALLY EXIST?

Over the past century billions of images of every part of human anatomy have been meticulously studied and used to guide internal surgeries. Magnetic, thermographic, and photographic images of "normal" are known.

There are times when an evil spirit can be "caught on camera". In my case, a demon was seen in an x-ray film of my back taken on a Friday. He is seen rather like a mouse sitting atop my pelvis at the lower lumbar. Prayer on Sunday removed him, as proved by a second x-ray taken the following Monday. I still have both x-ray films to prove it!

It came as an after-thought to print that image here. We set up the film against a backlight to photograph it. The result was imperfect but sufficient to reprint here for your examination. Skeptics will always find a reason to disbelieve, but this is a provable fact, attested by others who examined the film, including two chiropractors and a radiologist, in whose written report was that the "figure is of unknown etiology [origin]". He had not read this book!

In a similar incident, there was a middle-aged woman in our church in Chicago named Mildred, whom I knew well. Her body remained seriously twisted, even after 32 operations. At one point a demon named Spastic showed up in her x-ray in the form of a black snake wrapped around her spine. My good friend, Jerry Sodeman, while caring for Mildred and her husband, had tied her to himself with a rope to prevent her compulsive suicide attempts to jump out of an upstairs window while he slept. This is not a common occurrence, but it sometimes happens that imaging reveals spiritual entities. Often doctors admit they cannot explain it. In the case of my lower back x-ray, the doctor could not explain the "figure" seen and inscribed it with four arrows on the negative.

Newscasters often philosophically pose the question of evil - ironically while daily reporting its disease, distress, mayhem, war, death, and destruction in every nation on earth. Who could deny it? They might well ask, "Does good exist?" Fortunately, the Bible answers both questions with a resounding yes. But what is the source? Is evil caused by ourselves alone, or are there other causes?

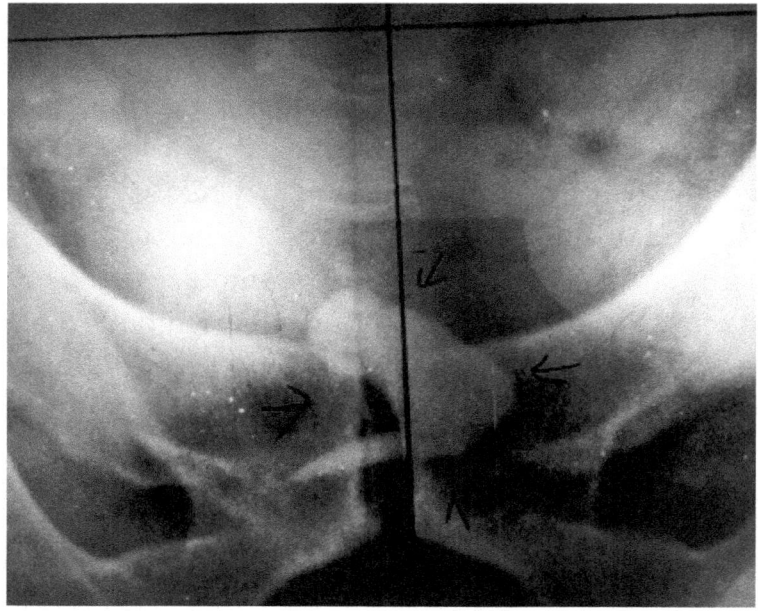

Figure 1 X-ray showing demon (mouse shape) by arrows

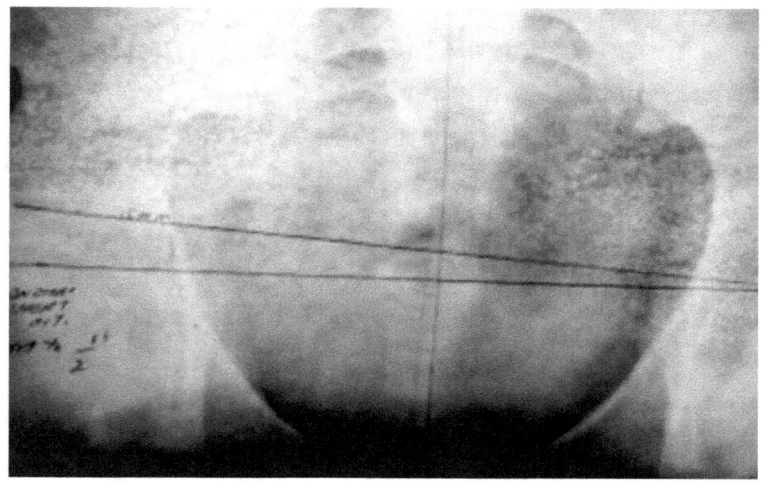

Figure 2 X-ray showing demon is gone

Yes, and yes. The out-of-control human nature craves to do evil, and resists anything contrary to itself. Good and evil forces have opposed each other in battle, beginning with the first human engagement with the devil. It is explained in Genesis 2:9; and 3:5+22 [Genesis means the origin]. You will notice that the three kinds of persons involved in the first episode were the only two humans in existence, one evil angel, and the Person of God. They all were in the Garden of Eden, conversing in human language in regard to the same event. The essence and result of their conversations soon necessitated the development of laws, courts of law, prisons, jails, hospitals, religions, and massively destructive weapons to be used by "hostiles" to steal, kill, and destroy. The exercise of their conflicting iron wills has rendered every living human helpless to prevent his own death. Except for divine intervention, this brief synopsis would have described the beginning and end of all human history.

The participants then and now are the same. By some measures some eight billion humans have died. We who now live through ongoing battles are estimated to be about seven and one half billion. We, too, shall die because of the same underlying reason - sin.

Satan's invisible minions and the Lord's angels are beyond number because spirits, once created, are immortal, which means that none of them has ever died. It is demonized humans and the [daemon] lower rank demon forces who are our main oppressors, and against whom we fight. The origin of demons has not been clearly revealed, which is why speculations abound. The Bible shows they are not aliens in the fashion of science fiction movie portrayals – such as vampires, humanoids, zombies, the living dead, avatars, half animal-half humans – Star Trek being a prime exhibitor of such. Rather, they are mobile spirits – invisible beings with all the characteristics of personhood. Some speculate they are the spirit remains of civilizations destroyed before Adamic humans were created, citing the opposite earth conditions described in the first two verses of Genesis. Scholar Derek Prince elaborated on this point in his book, War in Heaven. Some say that fallen angels are now demons, though the Bible states that the angels who rebelled are "reserved in everlasting chains under darkness unto the judgment of that great day" (Jude 6 and 2 Peter 2:4). These Scriptures undermine that speculation, though one teacher weakly postulates that only some evil angels are chained while others remain active on earth. I find little support for this notion.

A mixed species of giants was spawned by "sons of God" who rebelled by leaving their first estate [in the heavens, most believe] to mate with fair ladies on earth. Their proliferated offspring probably numbered in the millions before being destroyed under God's judgment of the famous flood in the days of Noah. Read about it in Genesis 6:1-7 and 9:19. With the physical gene pool of giants thereby destroyed, the adamic lineage was preserved to again repopulate through the eight-member family of righteous Noah, whose offspring we are. Not only did the unruly heavenly creatures admire earth's women, but ordinary men also consider fair ladies to be beautiful. Who could deny that? Many have received the unearned gift of beauty, which, though desirable, does not make any of them good, just attractive to the eyes of the wistful.

Through this account we see that at least one order of heavenly beings was able to transform themselves into human form sufficiently to reproduce a hybrid race by mating with women. We also learn that some angelic hosts have many of the same characteristics as humans, such as vision, will, desire, thought, speech, tendency to disobey God, and freedom to either remain in place, or to violate the borders of their assigned abode. Regardless of kind, however, the inescapable eternal-death consequence for disobedience is the same for us all. The one exceptional kind who are offered salvation from eternal death is the humankind, created specially and uniquely in God's image and likeness. All others perish without such an opportunity, for it was the Lord's choice to become a man - not an angel or spirit, to sacrificially pay the price exclusively for our salvation and for no other. He calls us his family (Ephesians 3:15).

The architect of pride, envy, and murder was archangel Lucifer. While in heaven, he and his followers could not reproduce themselves after their own kind, except in the matter of skewed morality. Pride produced self-will, which in turn caused Lucifer to break away from service and worship to God, in order that he might exalt himself to be above and "like the Most High" [Isaiah 14:12-14]. Scripture shows that any expressed will that is not also the will of God is an act of rebellion, which carries the penalty of eternal death. Jesus informed all humanity of that fact when he carefully phrased his instruction of what we are to pray to his Father: "Thy will be done in earth, as it is in heaven" [Matthew 6:10]. And in First Peter 5:6, "Humble yourselves under the mighty hand of God...". The most excruciating demonstration of yielding to God's will was Jesus in the Garden of Gethsemane, facing death by crucifixion, appealing to God, "... take away this cup from me: nevertheless, not what I will, but as thou wilt" (Mark14:36). This leaves no tolerance for expressions of the fatal self-will. For this we must be thankful, seeing the earthly chaos that all other wills have produced!

Below are biblical examples of non-human agents directly involved in human affairs. These help us understand how embellishments of facts have often mischaracterized invisible persons to the point of regarding them as mere mythology. Whether they be high rank, low level, good or evil in nature, they are indeed persons, who exhibit all the marks of personality. Psychologists define what constitutes a person as an entity who has mind, will, intellect, emotion, and speech. In all these respects, therefore, every such kind of them, including God, is a person whether living inside a physical body or not. All exert a measure of influence upon each human's mind, body, and activity. To emphasize the fact of their personhood, here are abbreviated quotations of Old and New Testament scriptures, beginning with the angelic, that manifest all the evidence of personality openly exhibited or clearly implied.

REFERENCES TO ARCHANGEL LUCIFER

- Genesis 3:2-5 In the form of a serpent he tempted Eve to sin.
- Job 1:6-7 Went from earth into a council of the Sons of God in heaven
- 1 Chronicles 21:1 Provoked David to sin by taking a census of Israel
- Matthew 4:1-11; Mark 1:12-13; and Luke 4:3-13 He tempted Jesus three times
- John 12:31 + 14:30 Satan is called prince of this world
- 1 Corinthians 5:1-5 Paul threatened a rebellious sinner with destruction by Satan

- 2 Corinthians 11:14-15 Satan and his ministers transformed into angels of light
- Ephesians 2:2 Satan called prince of the power of the air
- Ephesians 6:12 Satanic powers called rulers of the darkness of this world

VOICES OF DEMONS

- Matthew 8:28-29 and Mark 5:1-16 The demon Legion loudly proclaimed that Jesus is the Son of God.
- Mark 1:23-26 Unclean spirit in the man in Synagogue cried aloud, "Let us alone".
- Mark 9:17-26 A dumb and deaf demon cried aloud and came out of a boy
- Luke 4:33-34 Unclean demon spoke to Jesus in public, then obeyed and fled
- Acts 19:14-16 Demon said, "Jesus I know and Paul I know, but who are ye?" Then he leaped upon, assaulted and ripped the clothes off the imposters who fled naked and wounded.
- (Read Patty's testimony in Book One of 50+ others who gave us their names and activities.)

VOICE OF GOD

The thought-voice of God is a compelling urge that grabs full attention to do, say, or think something toward a desirable task, gift, or answer to prayer.

- Genesis 3:8-21 Had conversation with Adam, Eve, and Satan as serpent
- Exodus 33:11 Spoke to Moses face to face
- Matthew 3:17 Spoke from heaven that He was well pleased with Jesus
- Acts 9:5 Spoke from heaven to Saul of Tarsus on his way to Damascus
- 2 Corinthians 12:1-7 + Galatians 1:12 Took Paul into heaven to present the gospel

DREAMS, VISIONS, VOICES, AND ANGELS

- Genesis 15:1 "...word of the Lord came to Abram in a vision
- Numbers 20:16 Angel brought Israel out of Egypt
- 2 Samuel 24:15-16 Lord's angel kills 70,000 of David's men
- 1 Chronicles 21:18 Angel commanded Gad to speak to David
- Joel 2:28 Wrote that young and old would have dreams and see visions
- Genesis 6:4 Angelic sons of God came from heaven and married fair ladies
- Genesis 28:12-13 Angel spoke to Jacob in a dream
- Matthew 2:12 Wise men were warned of God in a dream
- Matthew 2:13 Angel appeared to Joseph in a dream

- Matthew 28:5 Angel attended the Tomb of Jesus and spoke to women
- Luke 1:27 Angel Gabriel spoke to Mary about conceiving baby Jesus
- Luke 2:9-11 Angel proclaimed to shepherds the birth of Jesus
- Acts 8:26 An angel spoke to Philip
- Acts 9:10-16 God spoke to Ananias in a vision about Saul's assignment
- Acts 10:1-3 Angel appeared to Apostle Peter and to Gentile Cornelius
- Acts 12:7-8 Angel broke chains off Peter, gave instructions, led him out of prison
- Acts 27:23-24 Angel stood by and talked to Apostle Paul
- Hebrews 1:13-14 Angels minister for heirs of salvation [followers of Christ].
- Revelation 1:1 Angel sent to give the Revelation to Apostle John
- Revelation 9:13-16 The sixth angel blew the trumpet to signal more angels

MENTAL ARMOR

Seminar Parts One and Two focus attention on the crucial importance of thoughts and imaginations which we allow into our mind. Speaking of man, Proverbs 23:7 states: "...as he thinketh in his heart, so is he." My personal thoughts are of little concern to you. But thoughts and imaginations in your mind are a most serious matter. Ephesians 6:12-17 lists seven pieces of spiritual armor we must use to prevent damage from demonic assaults. Verse 17 is specific to our present subject, naming mental armor as "the helmet of salvation". It is designed to protect the peace and well-being of our mind. The need for head armor is obvious as we see football players clashing on the field, or warring soldiers assaulting each other in battle.

Your mind and emotions are a private world available only to you, the Lord, and to some degree, Satan and his spirit princes. Apart from your willing participation, no one can do much to change them. You are the essential one who can obtain assistance through prayer to make any needed change in your secret thoughts and emotions. John 10:10 informs us that "The thief cometh not, but for to steal, and to kill, and to destroy: I am come that they [Christians] might have life, and that they might have it more abundantly." And in 1 John 3:8, "...the Son of God was manifested [in human flesh], that he might destroy the works of the devil." These two Scriptures interlock. You cannot enjoy the promised abundance unless the works of the devil are destroyed. Can these internally opposing conditions live together in the same mind? Yes, and they are in constant warfare against each other.

Many of God's elect experience torment through addictions, fears, and emotional trauma. The Bible tells us that "fear hath torment" [1 John 4:18]. In deliverance ministry, one of the most common spirits identified is fear, by name and character. The torment of fear is opposite to abundant life. It diminishes and overshadows what would otherwise be overall prosperity. Wealth brings no reprieve. Rich and poor alike desperately need relief from struggles and compulsions that drive bad behavior – even against one's own will. From the material standpoint some have the best of everything, but misery overtakes them in marriage, celebrity, business, health, and family relationships, never realizing its cause or remedy, due to spiritual blindness. Even the folks who are devoutly religious and loyal to Christ needlessly suffer "for lack of knowledge" [Hosea 4:6].

Galatians 5:22 tells us, "...the fruit of the Spirit is love, joy, peace, long-suffering [patience], gentleness, goodness, faith, meekness, temperance [self-control]; against such there is no law." This temperament constitutes the abundant life that Jesus promised. If these blessed qualities characterize your life, you are living the very best life that earth has to offer. To the degree it has escaped you, however, you do not have that wonderful life. Its provision did not come cheap. The narrow way of the unpopular Cross is not always pleasant and is often to the contrary. Misery comes not only to heathen who worship idols and demons, but to the righteous as well. Suffering by reason of mental, emotional, physical, or financial trauma often attends the righteous. When these conditions occur, they most often begin in our thought progressions. Preventable, long-standing problems are often hidden from public view, which may have been subtle in their beginning. Others cannot readily see the inner challenges another person faces. One may say to you, "I don't understand why I feel the way I do. I don't have the joy that God promised. Where is the joy of my salvation? I don't have it." What they are not saying is that they are tormented in their sleep at night. Their emotions rage and rule over them. Their thoughts often drive them uncontrollably. Fear paralyzes them. People do not give you the full picture of the things going on inside; indeed, they cannot. They will tell you something with reservation, if at all. Inhibitions are set up in social settings; people just cannot open up. Even spouse, doctor, pastor, psychiatrist, father, minister, and friend are kept at arm's length. Moreover, some things are impossible to communicate in mere vocabulary. Sometimes there are no words to describe the depth or nature of a suffering, or even a beauty in our spirit. We are limited in the use of words. Feeling is not conveyed in mere words. For example, I may tell you I stood on a sandy ocean beach looking over the infinite ocean, with bubbling water lapping at my feet on a clear sun-shiny day under a deep blue sky, enjoying the warm breeze. But you cannot feel it with me. You can only listen enviously as I describe what I'm feeling. You might somewhat relate to an opposite type of experience when once you were commanded to assault an enemy-held beachhead facing deadly machine gun fire and were wounded during the war ... admittedly not precisely the same as the ocean scene. But how do you feel? I give you a word, and you associate what your experience has been relative to that word. You say "sky". But what sky do I see? I'm a nightwalker. When I look up, I sometimes see rain clouds, other nights I see stars and the moon. You say, sky, and you see the sun shining on the horizon. So it is with something beautiful, or with something terrible, hateful, and ugly that may have affected you for decades. You cannot convey the emotional ugliness that blinds your mind, dulls your senses, terrifies you, and drives you to do or say things you wish you had not done or said. It is your private world locked inside. Yes, you can pray and reveal your heart to the Lord. He is beyond restrictive social settings, and besides, He is invisible, which makes it easy. To use a grisly example that emphasizes the point, most of us are shocked upon learning that a close associate, friend, or family member has just committed suicide, leaving no note of explanation. Most such victims had contemplated their self-murder in secret, never revealing their thoughts to anyone. Suicides who have had fame, fortune, celebrity, or notoriety are widely reported in the media, while the unknown majority are lumped together as matter-of-fact statistics. There are private things within folks which others are not permitted to know, you and I included.

THOUGHTS AND KNOWLEDGE

We ask again, how important are your thoughts? What you think and imagine determines the very quality of life you live. We need to set a high priority on personally evaluating them. Exactly what are thoughts? Where do they come from? A partial answer is: "...out of the abundance of the heart the mouth speaketh" (Matthew 12:34). Your mouth does not speak, however, until you have heard the thought prior to speaking it.

Thoughts are voices of someone speaking in your mind. The Lord has much to say about them, as do psychologists. A child under the age of one year has no intellectual thoughts, because rational thought presupposes that the mind is actually processing acquired knowledge. There must be knowledge before there is human thought.

While the brain is physical, the mind is spiritual. "Be renewed in the spirit of your mind" (Ephesians 4:23). As the processor of thoughts, the spiritual mind is capable of devising colossal supercomputers that mimic itself. It is a junior copy of God's mind, enabling us to create near miraculous things, such as artificial intelligence, super computers, robots, interplanetary vehicles, and more. Almighty,

Omniscient God has forever been the Reservoir of all knowledge, before, during, and after all ages of time. He benevolently shares bits of it with his human family, rather like a daddy delights in sharing appropriate levels and types of knowledge with his "inventive" daughters and sons. Archangel Michael, speaking on behalf of God, informs us through Daniel 12:4 long in advance, that "... knowledge shall be increased." I interpret that to mean increasingly released to us from Jesus Christ. "...by Him all things consist" (Colossians 1:16-17).

In the broadest sense, all knowledge is revelation from God, for He has always known all persons and things past and future from before humans were created. Colossians 2:3 tells us about the knowledge God has. "In whom are hid all the treasures of wisdom and knowledge". Obviously then, God knew all the details of spaceships, smart phones, television, atomic bombs, and things yet to be imparted to man (so that man may "discover" them). All was contained within the mind of God from eternity. Revelation 1:8 "I am Alpha and Omega, the beginning and the ending, saith the Lord, which is, and which was, and which is to come, the Almighty." (Also see John 16:30 and John 21:17). The Scripture as originally written contains exactly the clarity intended by God for man to comprehend. If passages are not obviously understandable, they are part of what God decided to keep secret (Deuteronomy 29:29). "They belong to the Lord our God".

Let the redeemed stop trying to "dig out God's secrets, mysteries or supposed "codes", and instead concentrate on obeying his clear commands. I Samuel 12:14 tells us to Obey His Voice; I Samuel 15:22 adds "To obey is better than sacrifice".

A sudden burst of divine revelation is often difficult to articulate in human language. It is best proved through writing its content and researching relevant scriptures to verify its source and value. This is required because our flawed soul still is in rehabilitation and is unable to absorb a high voltage spiritual shock in our spirit. I Thessalonians 5:21 instructs us to "Prove all things; hold fast that which is good." Too often the character of knowledge received supernaturally is tainted by its antichrist spirit not being discerned.

Thus, we see that beyond the earthly knowledge we acquire through smell, taste, touch, hearing, and sight, Christians have one additional Source. Our spirit is infused with God's Spirit when we are born again, through which he directly speaks to us, Spirit to spirit. Divine revelation is knowledge we could not get any other way. He accesses our mind any time He chooses, and suddenly, we have divine knowledge, wisdom, and understanding.

Such on-the-spot revelations can be

overwhelming. A speaker may be preaching a message he researched in Scripture, when suddenly God illumines his mind with a deeper layer of revelation. It might be oblique or unrelated to the sermon in progress. Regardless, it is breathtaking and more real than any other knowledge acquired, and more exciting because it did not come through human research. The listener senses it is revelation but does not realize that it just now came! The preacher rejoices in surprise, too, which makes it all the more blessed.

In the same way, much information can also be supernaturally imparted from Satan's forces. Remember, he was created in heaven and lived there with God for untold eons of eternity. Christians are warned not to seek fortune tellers, psychics, tarot card readers, wizards, or séances to talk to "the dead". When you participate in these forbidden activities you are actually talking to evil spirits. Yes, you can acquire startling information through such enquiries, but along with it receive bedeviling problems. Information received that way may or may not be accurate, but when unlawfully acquired it has negative consequences. Believers are supposed to gain knowledge through our five senses and through the written or spoken revelation from God.

HOW DOES THE DEVIL SPEAK TO US?

When information is received supernaturally, it is

imperative to assess it carefully. Revelations should be challenged. How quick we are to say, "God told me…". But was it He? With practice we are able to discern the voice of the Lord ["my sheep know my voice", Jesus said], and sometimes you can hear a voice that sounds like the Lord's but is not his. In Isaiah 14:14 Lucifer says, "…I will be like the Most High." How much like God will he be? He does not qualify lt. He says, "I will be like Him." Jesus explained, if it were possible, they shall deceive the very elect" (Matthew 24:24). Not everyone is designated as the very elect. There are many born again Christians who speak in languages given by the Holy Spirit, yet also hear from the devil, believing it to be the voice of the Lord! They may genuinely hear from God, too. But we are admonished to become mature through personally studying and being taught the Word of God by qualified teachers, to properly discern the spirits. We must "…try the spirits to [prove] whether they are of God (1John 4:1).

Barraging our mind with thought-voices, demons also induce drowsiness at inconvenient times. Do you ever get drowsy when reading your Bible? Or when driving your vehicle on the highway? Drowsiness can come upon you as a legitimate feeling, but it also may come at the wrong time. While writing this chapter I was about to fall asleep. I thought, "I can't go to sleep now. I'm feeling exhausted when I shouldn't be!" When drowsiness is untimely and not related to lack of sleep, fight it! It may feel normal even while surreptitiously being induced as a false symptom. Our bodies get tired. Our eyes want to rest. That is a right feeling at the proper time, when you are legitimately tired, but not after eight hours of sleep. Shake your head, stomp your feet, and walk around. If the drowsiness is out of sequence and at an inappropriate time, it is unnatural and not of God.

Satan is described as a serpent, "... more subtil [subtle] than any beast of the field" (Genesis 3:1). While he never requires sleep, he may trick you with the thought or feeling that you are sleepy. Our task is to rightly discern spirits. Experience has shown that Satan's main ploy is to speak his thought voice into your mind and get you to believe it is your own. In fact, you are his greatest disguise. He may also say in a certain way, "This is the Lord." And you might believe him! He may put a chill down your spine – a master at causing all manner of feelings. But feelings cannot be relied upon and are not the only calculus by which we discern spirits. When a voice comes with feelings, weigh it, measure it, and challenge it. When in doubt, you may verbally challenge the thought voice: "Are you from God? Do you confess that Jesus Christ is the Son of God come "to destroy the works of the Devil?" The first time I did that the demon growled back, calling me a dirty name, repeating it twice! The evil one who covered the throne of God knows the secrets of God's throne that, quite likely, no other creature knows. His emissaries have been taught by their master (See Ezekiel 28: 13-19). They know and respond to whatever degree of faith you exert against them. They will not depart voluntarily. Referencing I Corinthians 12:10, the gift of "discerning of spirits" helps you to rightly divide your thoughts, where they come from, who is speaking to you, and inducing the feelings you are experiencing, whether of pain or of ecstasy.

What is typically called the human or carnal nature is essentially the devil's nature. It was imparted by Satan and imported through his half-truth deception of Eve (See Genesis 3:6 and 22), and by Adam who "harkened unto the voice of thy wife" (verse 17). The only scriptural provision for the carnal man—the Adamic nature, is death. It cannot be changed, healed, or resurrected unto newness of life. At the onset of rebellion that nature was irrevocably destined for annihilation. It would temporarily remain as an abrasive tool to be used by the Lord in testing our loyalty to him. When God came to earth as Jesus Christ, he made a new creation of you upon the event of your salvation. Christians do not have a converted old nature, but a totally new one – called Christian, or "little Christs", identified with and characterized as that of Jesus Christ (2 Corinthians 5:17). As we accommodate it, we are to actively "put off" the old and put on the new, through the abrasive process of repentance, praise, fellowship, and righteous service to others. This new creation is not a blend of the old and new mixed together. Rather, each nature remains distinctly separate while residing in the same "house", each one at war with the other. The old and new co-exist only while we live on earth. Our physical death separates them forever. This warfare is total and comprehensive, which we describe as "War of the World, Flesh, and the Devil".

Our heritage of Adam's fallen nature is the seedbed of evil that besets us. There are at least 32 adjectives in the King James translation to describe the fallen nature – the old man. Referring to it, Jesus said, "There is none good. No, not one" (Matthew 19:17). Contrary to what we like to believe, there is no good in anyone apart from the implanted nature of Jesus Christ.

Remove the divine constraints from man and you have a savage; one who would wantonly kill and deceive without cause. Beasts of the field kill prey for food and fight to reproduce their species. Unlike guiltless animals, however, man inherently expresses his depravity, greed and selfishness, as described and demonstrated throughout Scripture. Yet, in mercy, the Lord offers us one, and only one, way of salvation to those who accept it on His terms. That Way is through the blood of Jesus Christ.

GOD'S THOUGHTS

Psalm 40:5 says, "Many, O Lord my God, are thy wonderful works which thou hast done, and thy thoughts which are to us-ward: they cannot be reckoned up in order unto thee: if I would declare and speak of them, they are more than can be numbered." What is the Lord telling us here? The Bible says that God thinks, and God is thinking thoughts in David's mind. This is the usual way the Lord and we communicate, as we "...put on the mind of Christ" (1 Corinthians 2:16). Psalm 40, verse 17: "But I am poor and needy; yet the Lord thinketh upon me: thou art my help and my deliverer; make no tarrying, O my God." Here the Lord has continued thinking thoughts. Created in God's image and likeness, man thinks similarly in kind, but – on a much smaller scale! That is, we are "likeminded" [Romans 15:5 and Philippians 2:2+5].

Psalm 139:17 reconfirms it. "How precious also are thy thoughts unto me, O God! How great is the sum of them!" Through the mouth of David, God is telling us that God's thoughts are inside David's mind, and David is delighted with them.

Prophet Isaiah 55:8, "For my thoughts are not your thoughts, neither are your ways my ways, saith the Lord." This is not a contradiction of terms. God has His own thoughts, separate from ours, and He can think them in our mind as he chooses. Verse 9, "For as the heavens are higher than the earth, so are my ways higher than your ways, and my thoughts than your thoughts." Bless God. Who would doubt that? God has thought conversations with our thoughts inside our own mind! Again, he tells us in Jeremiah 29:11, "For I know the thoughts that I think toward you, saith the Lord, thoughts of peace, and not of evil, to give you an expected end." God is thinking thoughts toward you! Praise the Lord! How wonderful is that?!

I remember my late wife once musing in jest: "There you go thinking again!" To which I replied, "No, that was the mind of Christ thinking!" Love prevailed – I think!

MAN'S THOUGHTS

The above scriptures reveal a few of God's thoughts. Now let us look at man's thoughts. First Corinthians 3:20 says, "The Lord knoweth the thoughts of the wise, that they are vain." Psalm 50:21 says, "These things hast thou done, and I kept silence; thou thoughtest that I was altogether such an one as thyself: but I will reprove thee, and set them in order before thine eyes." The 'thou' above is God. Psalm 139:23 says, "Search me, O God, and know my heart: try me, and know my thoughts." Man is thinking thoughts and God knows all about them.

Proverb 23:7 says, "For as he [man] thinketh in his heart, so is he: Eat and drink, saith he to thee; but his heart is not with thee."

Proverb 24:9 says, "The thought of foolishness is sin: and the scorner is an abomination to men." Not only are foolish acts sin, but even a thought of foolishness is a sin! Matthew 9:4 says, "And Jesus knowing their thoughts said, wherefore think ye evil in your hearts?" Jesus is discerning in this case. He knows the unspoken thoughts of all people. Should we not be careful in what we choose to think?

Consider the most often used expression of insecure newsmen, journalists, and preachers alike. Try to count the times they say, "I think" or "I believe". Is that not troublesome? Apparently, they are not absolutely certain of anything. Yet they boldly declare their unqualified opinion to be positively the truth. Why would they not say, "I know as an absolute certainty that … such and such is so, and I stake my life on it!?" Sometimes your reputation, employment, or eternal destiny may hinge on your reliance upon what they say. No judgment is passed here, but it is valid to ask questions and to expect accountability, because "The eyes of the Lord run to and fro throughout the whole earth…" evaluating us (2 Chronicles 16:9).

HOW IMPORTANT ARE YOUR THOUGHTS?

"Let the words of my mouth and the meditation of my heart, be acceptable in thy sight, O Lord, my strength, and my redeemer" (Psalm 19:14)

The character of our thoughts determines the level of our blessing or cursing. Both good and evil forces use them as weapons of war. We are stuck with the need to fight mental-spiritual battles because our actions are driven by thinking thoughts, without which, our mind would not function. To the degree it incorrectly processes them is a liability. Characterizing that fact are unfortunate folks variously described as Idiot, Brain dead, Stupid, Crazy, Dim Wit, Dull minded, Simpleton, Insane, etc.

Mental malfunctions often are the direct result of demonic interference in the function of our mind and/or brain circuitry. Moreover, the human body, when operated by an impaired mind or brain, often produces seizures, palsy, speech impediments, migraine, confusion, and numerous other maladies. This problem is more fully presented in later pages and confirmed in Bible passages that describe the earthly ministry of Jesus Christ and his disciples.

Man is normally able to select what his mind thinks. He may permit or reject thought voices. Genesis 3:1-5 describes Eve's conversation with Satan but does not state that their words were spoken audibly. Satan is described there as a serpent, seemingly in bodily form. Basically, serpents do not talk to people. They just strike. Yet the Bible exactly quotes Satan and Eve's highly consequential conversation. I am suggesting that on that occasion

Satan might have been talking with Eve as he does with us today—inside our mind, while also inducing corresponding feelings and emotional impulses. That is also a primary way that God speaks to us. Whether audible or not, however, you can reason with a voice, you can counter it, you can contradict it, you can rebuke it, or you can entertain it. Satan and his princes are not able to speak audibly because they do not have vocal cords of a physical body. Yet they speak in thoughts almost without ceasing. They can also become somewhat visible in shadowy or ghostly form, which I have seen several times. They can make deals or covenants with men. But this is not as extant in our enlightened society as it is in undeveloped cultures that practice demon worship. Spirit Princes sometimes make an appearance in the form of brilliant light - a "wonder"; or an "apparition", of which there are many, seeking worship, or causing fear through their deceptions.

Eve was beguiled by Satan-the-serpent as she engaged him in apparently secret conversation separate from her husband – not a good idea. Second Peter 2:16 reveals that God made Prophet Baalam's four-legged beast to speak aloud in human language as a warning to the prophet. The Lord could likewise have allowed a physical serpent to similarly speak aloud. That distinction is not made clear on the occasion of Eve's visitation.

Ultimately, thoughts of disobedience to God's

Word are either from spirits of the devil or from the evil heart our old nature inherited from father Adam – who had made himself subservient to the devil. In James 3:15 that nature is called "devilish" and in Jeremiah 17:9 "deceitful and wicked". Often the question is asked, "How do I know whether it's me thinking or it's the devil?" It does not make much difference. Any thought of disobedience to God's Word is sin (Hebrews 4:12). Likewise, "The thought of foolishness is sin:" [Proverbs 24:9]. Thoughts are either of godly character or they are of disobedience. In that respect their exact source is immaterial. Universally there is blessing for obedience and cursing for disobedience. As we read in 2 Chronicles 19:7b, the Lord does not have special respect for any person; all are treated justly under the same rules of love and justice.

First Corinthians 13:5 tells us that love thinks no evil. "[Love] doth not behave itself unseemly, seeketh not her own, is not easily provoked, thinketh no evil." First John 4:8 says God is love. "He that loveth not knoweth not God; for God is love." God thinks no evil. If you have an evil thought at any time, it will not be from God. To define evil, go to Scripture! Any thought that is contrary to what Scripture prescribes "cometh of evil" (James 5:12). Philippians 4:8 says, "Finally brethren, whatsoever things are true, whatsoever things are honest, whatsoever things are just, whatsoever things are pure, whatsoever things are lovely, whatsoever things are of good report, if there be any virtue, and if there be any praise, think on these things." This is the quality of thought-life that Christians are commanded to embrace. Experience proves that carefully directed thinking is not so easy as it might seem. A new and higher level of concentration is required to restrict what is allowed into our mind and that effort needs constant attention. If you have any doubt about its difficulty, you might want to try it for a month. If you keep a tally sheet and mark each time your guard slips, prepare yourself for a shock! That is the moment you would see – perhaps for the first time – how entrenched your personal War of the World, the Flesh, and the Devil has been. It is more expedient to forestall a wrong thought than to remedy careless words that cause damage. That is the level of purity here advanced. Are you up to the task? Or at least to make the effort?

VOICES

First Corinthians 14:10 says, "There are, it may be, so many kinds of voices in the world, and none of them is without signification [significance]." This refers to more than your smart phone and television set perpetually blaring with voices. Psychiatrists well know the kinds of voices that are most problematic. They are the ones you hear inside your mind, those which no one else can hear. They are the loud, jangling, upsetting, tormenting demon voices, made more destructive when carried by voodoo drumbeats of music – so called. The seriousness of our thoughts and imaginations cannot be overemphasized as they are the rudder that guides us in every matter of life.

Second Corinthians 10:3-5 says, "For though we walk in the flesh, we do not war after the flesh. (For the weapons of our warfare are not carnal but mighty through God to the pulling down of strongholds;) Casting down imaginations and every high thing that exalteth itself against the knowledge of God and bringing into captivity every thought to the obedience of Christ."

These weapons are invisible but are mighty and supernaturally powerful. Wielding them enables us to defeat our adversary. What obedience are we talking about? The standard, again, is Philippians 4:8. If the character of your thought is not true, honest, just, pure, lovely, of good report, virtuous, or if there is no praise—take it captive! Do not permit it to speak. Cast it down. Command it to depart in Jesus' name.

Notice two other verses: Proverbs 13:3 says, "He that keepeth his mouth keepeth his life: but he that openeth wide his lips shall have destruction". Proverbs 17:27 says, "He that hath knowledge spareth his words: and a man of understanding is of an excellent spirit." Proverbs 21:23 says, "Whoso keepeth his mouth and his tongue keepeth his soul from troubles". These passages emphasize watching not only the words that flow out of our mouth but necessarily include the thoughts that precede the words that are spoken.

Matthew 5:37 says, "But let your communication be, Yea, yea; Nay, nay: for whatsoever is more than these cometh of evil." You say "Yes," and you say "No." Jesus says that anything more tends to come from an evil source. There was a time when I questioned that, but when put together with other scriptures it makes sense. The Lord is saying, be quiet and listen. Say yes and say no. Why? Because the heart is full of evil and deceit and is desperately wicked (Jeremiah 17:9). Who can know it? The Lord alone.

James 1:26 says, "If any man among you seem to be religious, and bridleth not his tongue, but deceiveth his own heart, this man's religion is vain." I am convinced that Jesus was a quiet man for the most part. He would not repeatedly give us these instructions with such frequency in both the Old and New Testaments unless he had practiced what he preached. He was alone much of the time. Not only so, in Isaiah 53:2, we are shown that "…he hath no form nor comeliness; and when we shall see him, there is no beauty that we should desire him."

This shows that Jesus was not humanly handsome, even though irresistibly magnetic because he presented hard truth with love. Why is it that artisans and sculptors unfittingly make Jesus to look beautiful?

IMAGINATIONS: ADVANCED THOUGHTS

Fantasies. Fables. Television. Movies. Scripture uses the word fable five times. Webster's Dictionary defines fable as: "a fictitious story, a myth, a legend, or falsehood." Television and movie productions essentially are fiction, myths, legends, and falsehoods. Through them, a demon named Pretense enters into many of us. I was immersed eight years in the movie business and was fortunate to have expelled that very demon, along with six others in a small public meeting. He departed out of me in a prolonged, high-pitched squeal, through ministry of my friend, Cas Knoester, missionary to Kenya.

Fables are not projected only through television and movies. Nursery schools teach rhymes and tales of imaginary creatures such as Cinderella, Grimm's Fairy Tales, and more. Another door is opened for evil spirits to enter when teachers require the reading of Harry Potter novels about magical feats. Young children are thereby jeopardized. In 2 Timothy 4:3-4 we are warned: "For the time will come when they will not endure sound doctrine, but after their own lusts shall they heap to themselves teachers, having itching ears; And [teachers] shall turn away their [children's] ears from the truth, and shall be turned unto fables."

When Bible truth is removed from schools [or churches], all that is left is the crass earthly knowledge of fables and lies. One such is the lie of evolution, that contradicts the biblical account of creation. Propagated universally, such fables make it difficult to get people to talk about things that are verifiably true. Indoctrinated by the world system of propaganda, they would rather "laugh their way to hell". Does this sound radical? Yes, and Jesus also was radical.

FABLES AND FANTASIES

As progenitor of evil, Satan engaged Eve to present a toxic mixture that included a portion of truth. For what purpose? The partial truth deceived her and brought her under his bondage in slavery. His tactic is to mix truth with lies, a deadly cocktail that has worked for him throughout all human existence. In Genesis 3:4-5 we read: "And the serpent said unto the woman, Ye shall not surely die: for God doth know that in the day ye eat thereof, then your eyes shall be opened, and ye shall be as gods, knowing good and evil." Notice in verse 22 that the Lord confirmed as true only the last part of what Satan had told her: "... Behold, the man is become as one of us, to know good and evil...". A half - truth is a whole lie. It may be called a fairy tale, or fable, such as those taught to children in elementary school. That is where children's minds are programmed to later receive more complex deceptions. A half-truth is the most insidious form of lying and is equal to murder in God's eyes. "...all liars shall have their part in the lake which burneth with fire and brimstone" (Revelation 21:8).

ENHANCED THOUGHTS

An imagination is a thought that has been pondered, entertained, and advanced to a pattern, image, design, fantasy, or plan. It begins as a simple thought, which progresses toward a plan of action, unless challenged: Philippians 4:10: "...[bring] every thought into captivity unto the obedience of Christ." Thoughts must be stopped and evaluated as they begin to enter into our mind. If one is impure, do not wait until it becomes a full-blown imagination, for it may capture you if you fail to take it captive. Yes, you might be able to take authority over it at the later point, but it is wiser to discern the spirit of it before it goes that far. Why give the devil free use of your mind? Challenge thoughts at their very onset. Bring them into captivity under the obedience of Christ. Assure that your thoughts are pure. If you wait until an unholy thought has stirred a fire of latent lust, you will be trapped in a full-blown imagination that is sure to cause you trouble. The devil will take command of your mind to the degree you permit him. He will interject perverse thoughts, evil images, and unclean pictures in your mind. That includes the memories of past sins that are ugly enough to make you wince in disgust. Shut them out; tell him they are none of his business, and he should go tell it to Jesus, who absolved us of all such things on our behalf. Our task is to recognize the evil source before he gains a foothold to distort truth and disturb our peace.

By training yourself to habitually challenge each thought, within a year you will become adept at it. You will be able to stop it in its tracks the moment it begins to enter your mind. But you have to be quiet enough in your spirit to listen and evaluate it. Remember the Scripture phrase: "a meek and quiet spirit…is of great price in the sight of God" (1 Peter 3:4).

No doubt you have heard of Santa Claus. That fantasy falls into the fable category.

One day in late December the Holy Spirit spoke very clearly to me in Van Nuys, California. George Otis and I were driving on Victory Boulevard. Suddenly, I stated what had instantly flashed into my mind: "Santa is Satan; S-A-N-T-A | S-A-T-A-N." With an audible gasp, George Otis exclaimed his understanding … "DAVID!!" It was breathtaking. God began to unfold how that Christians everywhere honor Santa Claus in their homes and churches. Who is Santa Claus? Matthew 7:20 says, "By their fruit, ye shall know them." Satan | Santa—same spelling with just one letter transposed - and not by chance. Notice the truly divine characteristics which Santa-Satan abrogates to himself, remembering he had said, "I will be like the MOST HIGH" (Isaiah 14:14).

Satan | Santa comes from the "sides of the North". He comes on the day that celebrates Christ, wearing red and white colors that represent Christ's Blood and purity. He comes to bring "good" gifts to men, just like the wise men brought gifts to Jesus after His birth. James 1:17 reveals that "Every good gift comes down from God, the Father of lights..." Santa usurps the position of Jesus who was the greatest Gift given to mankind, to bring good gifts to the children of men. He supposedly even knows where you are, and he comes to you in America and to peoples across the world all within one night, imitating and mocking God's omniscience and omnipresence.

Santa has songs that exalt him and his greatness—"he knows when you are sleeping, he knows when you are awake, he knows if you have been bad or good, so be good for goodness sake". Only almighty God is omniscient. He knows all things, at all times, and in all places. But does Santa Claus? Really? "I will be like the Most High." He comes down from the sky above and propagates his lie. Children see their indulgent parents pretending to be Santa Claus bringing them gifts. The children may soon figure it out, but the farce will have undermined their faith in the truth of Scripture. Santa Claus replaces Jesus. Yet, Santa Claus is anti-Christ. He is Satan. He is just one more tool the devil uses to slap Jesus in the face, targeting children. Remember, Satan cannot hurt the Lord Jesus Christ directly, but dares to use his false image in mockery of Christ.

Satan has access to talk with God and is a false accuser. Revelation 12:10 plainly states: "...for the accuser of our brethren is cast down, which accused them [believers] before our God day and night." In Job 1:6-7 Satan presented himself before the Lord.

Fairytales, Santa Claus, the devil. One might carry the point further and talk about Easter also. The resurrection of the Lord Jesus Christ is (dis)honored by Ishtar, a false goddess. "Ishtar" is literally "Easter" and is worshiped as the mother of God and Queen of Heaven. While there is no holiday prescribed in Scripture to celebrate Jesus' birthday or resurrection, celebrations nonetheless have become an expression of the heart for many believers. Romans 14:5 makes allowance for some to celebrate one day over another for reasons of conscience: "One-man esteemeth one day above another: another esteemeth every day alike. Let every man be fully persuaded in his own mind." Thus, we find celebrations by many whose motive, in good conscience, is pure toward God. The obvious excesses that pollute such observances, however, should be avoided.

We are examining the deceiver and how he so easily deceives us. Have you ever been deceived by him? I have, more than once. Uncovering his tactics helps prepare us for warfare against him, moment-by-moment. Challenging your thoughts is not a one-time episode but is an ongoing, life-enhancing process. It needs to become our way of life. Its practice should become so indelibly inculcated in our mind that we never forget to challenge every thought, testing them against the measuring rod of Philippians 4:8, quoted above. If you are going to have victory over the devil in your personal life, and in your home, you have to do this! There is no short-cut, no substitute. No one can do it for you. Ask the Holy Spirit to help you, and He will.

MUTUAL HERITAGE

"And God saw that the wickedness of man was great in the earth, and that every imagination of the thoughts of [man's] heart was only evil continually" (Genesis 6:5). "And the Lord said, Behold, the people is one, and they have all one language; and this they begin to do: and now imagined to do" (Genesis 11:6).

First Chronicles 28:9, "...the Lord searcheth all hearts, and understandeth all the imaginations of the thoughts: if thou seek him, he will be found of thee; but if thou for-sake him, he will cast thee off forever."

Psalm 38:12, "They also that seek after my life lay snares for me: and they that seek my hurt speak mischievous things and imagine deceits all day long."

Romans 1:21, "...[they] became vain in their imaginations, and their foolish heart was darkened."

Think of your mind as a television receiving

set whose controller is in your hand. As it is with television, so it is with your mind – the thought receiver. To get the clearest image and sound we must change the channel to the Lord's signal. Doing so will set the stage for illumination and revelation of the right kind. This presumes, of course, that you are in charge of yourself. If you find that you cannot control your thoughts, you need deliverance, because if you are not in control, someone else surely is – and he must be cast down and out.

In the warfare arena we must understand how to stay free, once delivered from evil spirits.

How do we keep them out? How do the spirits act? How do you detect evil spirits returning?

Hate was a spirit "strongman" in my life for many years. It does not mean that I consciously hated. It just means that for 41 years, I had an internally resident spirit of hate that drove me, and I did not know it. He was the last of six who were expelled from me in Dallas, Texas. I do not find it difficult to hate and must carefully guard against it. There are things to hate if you want to do so. I do hate the devil. I hate every demon who ever oppressed me. There is nothing good about them. Jesus does not love them either.

Our reference to 'Satan' includes his hierarchy of demons who populate the earth and its environs. It is their mission to destroy humans made in the image of God. There are only three Scripture examples I find where Satan personally visited the earth, and only two where he verbally spoke to man. His first speaking was to Eve in the garden of Eden (see Genesis 3:1-5), and his second was to Jesus Christ in the wilderness of temptation (See Matthew 4:3-10).

CHAPTER SIX

HOW TO KEEP YOUR DELIVERANCE

Primarily he operates through his demon princes who are assigned a geographic domain, such as: Prince of Persia, the Prince of New Orleans, Prince of Liverpool England, or the Prince of Guatemala, for example. They in turn rule over spirits of lesser power within their domain. Their structure is similar to military rankings—the higher the rank, the greater the number of soldiers who take orders from them. Here we mostly refer to lower rank demons. Satan dictates strategy to his princes, who must execute it through their descending ranks – as do armies of nations with officers, sergeants, corporals, and privates. Generally, it is the lower ranks who manifest in direct battle with humans.

Interaction with spirit entities reveals their

varying degrees of power. It may require more effort to evict a higher rank spirit ("strong man") than one of low rank. In the Dallas, Texas deliverance referred to above, the last of six spirits to depart was named Hate. He was the "strongman" in charge of a particular group. Demons do not usually operate alone but work in packs under authority of the strongman in charge. You may recognize the term "wolfpack", often used to describe a pack of attack animals, as well as referencing groups of Nazi submarine ships of World War II. It is an apt description for a gang of demons also.

How do you deal with the devil? How does he deal with us? He may be compared to a bully. A bully will bluff and push as much as you permit him. A bully will make a fool out of you if you let him. If you do not defend yourself, he will keep slapping you around. If you are a meek or acquiescent victim, you will start to believe the bully is stronger than he really is. Hopefully there will come a day when you have had enough! On that day he will have slapped you for the last time. Having nothing more to lose, you turn around and bash his face as hard as you can. When you do that, he will be afraid to attack you again. Why? Because a bully never wants to take on a fighter! You will notice that a bully never oppresses someone twice his size—quite the opposite. He is a coward. When a smaller person becomes courageous, he can defeat a bully – first blurring his eyesight, then beating his face. A defeated bully ceases to be a bully. So, it is with demons who are suddenly made to fear the power of Jesus in us.

HARD THINGS

Some folks have said, "You are hard". It is not wrong to be hard, but hard how? Hard against the adversary! In fact, you will not find a dedicated deliverance minister who has not been seasoned with the quality of hardness. The common denominator is a deep-down quality of hardness beyond which he will not be pushed by demons. Such ministers have dealt too long with too many people who were overrun by evil spirits tormenting their person and families. A soft wimp does not dare to teach or do spiritually hard things, especially casting out demons, and more especially do so in a public forum.

There are notable examples of the hardness of Jesus, the Carpenter who developed strong muscles building perfect furniture, the One who looked squarely into the eyes of his nation's supreme court judges while calling them hypocrites, whited sepulchers full of dead men's bones. He did not mince words, was not cowardly, but was a hard man in the right sense of the word. We are to follow his example. Merchants in the temple who were doing what they thought was a good thing (selling birds and animals to be sacrificed inside the synagogue of God) were suddenly on the receiving end of the whip

Jesus made as He turned over their tables and drove them off. He was not a soft, feminine or emasculated Deliverer, as is so often displayed on a decorative cross and expressed in mushy Christianity. That is not the real Jesus. He was a strong man, saying, in paraphrase, "Nobody takes My life from Me, I lay it down" (John 10:17-18). Neither Pontius Pilate nor Satan had the power to kill this perfect Man. Neither were his twelve newly-energized disciples weak – except for traitor Judas Iscariot, after Satan had "entered into him" (Luke 22:3). Satan makes one cowardly.

Jesus was hard when it came to issues that deserved hardness, yet He also was, and remains, compassionate, loving, and tender toward needy individuals. A man of emotion, He wept. As tender as His love was, He was just as hard and steely when it came to self-righteous hypocrites. Jesus never backed down from any man, woman, Satan himself, or from difficult circumstances.

His gospel also is hard. He says, "Take up your cross and follow me." You ask, "Where will it take me, Lord?" Where did it take Him? It took Him to the death of Himself. Do you remember Gethsemane? Jesus asked the disciples to pray with Him awhile. They were tired and weary. Jesus called out, "O my Father, if it is possible, let this cup pass from me: nevertheless, not as I will, but as thou wilt" (Matthew 26:39 and Luke 22:42). This was an unspeakably hard place. Talk about a hard decision that had to be made by Jesus, a man of flesh and bone. The Bible says He went back to the rock altar the second and third time, fervently praying with great drops of sweat and blood, asking Father God if there was another way.

We are admonished to do similar things that develop us into the same character as seen in Jesus. We have to grow up into it, step-by-step, stage-by-stage, victory-by-victory, and sometimes defeat-by-defeat, for the sake of what we believe to be right. We have to trust God to bring us out of unholy circumstances. We are sometimes snared in ignorance, through deceit, and sometimes by yielding to temptations of the world, flesh, or the devil.

Every Christian is subject to the "downward pull". Multitudes fall. If it were not so, there would have been no need for God to repeatedly warn, "Be sober, be vigilant: because your adversary the devil, as a roaring lion, walketh about, seeking whom he may devour…whom resist steadfast in the faith…" (1 Peter 5:8-9). Beware of him! We are to stand against the wiles of the devil. Put on the whole armor of God: the helmet of salvation, the breastplate of righteousness, the all-important shield of faith, your feet shod with the preparation of the gospel of peace, gird up our loins with truth. All those pieces of armor are essential for protection, but there is one other that is even more potent.

The devil is not afraid of your shield, helmet, buckled belt, shoes, or girded loins. But he is afraid of your sword, the Rhema of God—the living, vital, dynamic, powerful Word of God, which must be lived, meditated upon, memorized, spoken, and commanded. The Word of God destroys the works of the devil when offensively wielded. (Read Ephesians chapter six). The Sword of the Spirit (the Word of God) is the only attack weapon listed – It is our one and only offensive piece of armor.

The best way to defend yourself from the devil is to attack him. This was true for me more than once under concerted attack, when there was no other defense and no helper in sight. It is best, however, to engage with other warrior brothers and sisters in fellowship rather than go it alone. We need to study the Word of God by every means to sharpen and keep that two-edged sword ready to wield. We can count on Satan to counterattack in force. It is a law of the devil and his wolfpacks: steal, kill, and destroy.

During World War II, commandos and marines would deploy to retake an island overrun by the enemy. The first thing they would do after establishing a beachhead was get out their shovel and dig in. Why? Because they knew the enemy would counterattack. This is a clear picture of what it means to take a beachhead in spiritual battles.

Your first deliverance establishes a little beachhead. It is the first step to secure your island, but certainly not victory over the whole warfront. Your first deliverance is a battle you won, a skirmish. There will be more battles to fight.

How do you dig in for the counterattack? It is spiritual, and recognizable in your soul -- emotions and thoughts. The counterattack can also be an affliction in your body or in negative circumstances. It can be all of these at once, subtly coming at you from seemingly unrelated sources. Nothing that happens in total war, however, is unrelated to the overall strategy. Each battle is integral to a master plan designed to defeat the opposition.

Realize that Satan's greatest weapon is secrecy. If he can keep you from recognizing him, he is a long stride forward in making you yield. He does not throw everything at you at once. Again, using the military metaphor, he uses snipers with telescopic, silenced rifles hidden atop a distant coconut palm tree. They will zero in and fire a single shot so you cannot determine their location. He will stay hidden, come in subtly, one little maneuver at a time, to cause you to believe your calculated calamity is a "natural" happening.

It may be as rudimentary as your son suddenly falling and dislocating his kneecap. You rush him to the emergency room, asking the Lord to help. That is proper. But you may not recognize it was likely caused by Satan's trickery. Or your teenage daughter uncharacteristically takes up with an unruly boy. Your refrigerator fails to cool, and the food inside will spoil if you cannot quickly get it fixed. You are frustrated five times in one morning and start thinking negative thoughts about yourself and others. Your boss blindsides you with someone's accusation that has no basis in truth. Little things one after the other. That is the time to stop everything for a moment and recognize that these "anomalies" were a set-up of the enemy in counterattack mode! Negative things which seem to be natural are often manipulations by our invisible, supernatural enemy.

There are obvious and not-so-obvious ways to keep your deliverance. Let us examine both. Suppose that you have been delivered of a spirit named Envy. All your life you had a problem with Envy. You did not recognize that this disturbing personality trait was the aggravation of an evil spirit until after you were somewhere between 30 and 75 years old. Looking at your life in retrospect, you recall that even as a youth, you envied the boy in junior high school whose wealthy father gave him a new Buick car on his 16th birthday. You did not have a car. You had to bum around with friends and share the cost of gas for their jalopy. As an adult, you remember that you had coveted the car he had and envied him having it, wishing you could have one, too. You remember seeing other expensive automobiles over the years, especially that Silver Cloud Rolls Royce model. Somehow the details of that Rolls Royce stuck in your mind. You coveted it and you envied the lucky guy who drove it.

You remember Aunt Susie who married the wealthy doctor who gave her everything she desired. Oh, they had their marital problems, but materially they were well off. You, on the other hand, did not marry so well. Your income was average. You married the right person, but you did not have costly possessions. Resentment developed. They had more than you and you did not like it. You coveted what they had and envied your Aunt Susie's good fortune.

Looking back, you may now see that you have always had a tendency to envy – a weakness of character. God is showing you it has been a real problem for you. You may have said to yourself, "It's the way I've always been. Isn't everybody like this?"

No, not exactly. Your coveting is bad, but no worse than my hate problem was. Now, with the Envy spirit expelled, it is time for you to dig in. The counterattack is eminent. You may again be experiencing the same type of envy you had all of your life, though now being induced from the outside. The devil tells you the deliverance "didn't take". He is a liar. I am saying that you were delivered! It may take a while to fully realize it experientially. It can take from weeks to a year to fully assess all that God has done for you in a deliverance – especially if it was major and multiple.

Once you have asked God to deliver you, and have received prayer for deliverance, dare not say, "I received nothing." That contradicts God's Word of promise; He does not tell lies. You cannot know all that was accomplished in the spirit realm. The fact is, "Ask and it shall be given you; seek, and ye shall find; knock, and it shall be opened unto you" (Matthew 7:7). It is your Father's good pleasure to give you the kingdom. If you are looking for a particular kind of experience, evidence, or manifestation, you may not see it. But do not contradict God's Word. If you experience an immediate evidence or manifestation, praise the Lord! But feelings and manifestations are not an ironclad requirement, even though on most occasions an expulsion will be evident.

After my first deliverance there were two weeks of decreasing pressures, enough for me to know there had suddenly been a dramatic change in my life. There had been no manifestation at the time of prayer, and I had no other way of knowing until the problem abated. Likewise, give yourself time to evaluate and consolidate changes in your feelings, actions, reactions, and motivations. Soon enough you will become convinced that the Lord was faithful in helping you. We exercise faith first — before seeing its result. A former associate, Rodney Lynch, often said of spiritual things, "We have not been this way before!"

No matter what spirit you have been delivered

from, carefully watch for the undesirable trait or action to reappear subtly. If the deposed demon can approach you unaware, he will repeatedly return, probing for a way to reenter your life. He evaluates the degree to which you overlook his deception. Fix in your mind that He is an undying, implacable foe. Be ever alert, never caught off guard.

In continuous warfare it is your solid faith beyond good words that hinders him. If you are not aware of him, you cannot resist him. He wants you to believe your deliverance did not happen. God says a change will have been made, whether you have fully realized it or not. Satan's approach is through feelings, direct thoughts he induces, and images he flashes onto the screen of your mind. Remember that Rolls Royce? For some reason a shiny El Dorado Cadillac will pass you on the street and you think, "Gee, that's a better car than I have." Then Satan comes in and flashes, "Rolls Royce." Now your mind sees the object of your obsession – the Rolls Royce! Do you see the careful, subtle progression? You saw the Cadillac. Your mind was not on anything in particular. You may be speaking in tongues and singing praises to the Lord, when suddenly a glint from the shiny chrome of a Cadillac crosses your line of vision. One quick glance at it and Satan whispers, "Rolls Royce."

He hits your weak spot. You may experience a flash of tightness in your stomach, or nausea may develop. There will be a persistent stirring. The slightest feeling or thought in the direction of your lifetime weakness is the thing that will most likely trip you up. Remain alert for any subtle approach of the devil. As in every kind of warfare, live in readiness and be on guard. Obviously, this principle applies to any and every aspect of the carnal nature, not just lust for money and things. If you are taken in a fault, blame no one but yourself. Satan is just doing his ordinary work. Repent, ask forgiveness, then "go and sin no more" (See I John 1:9-10). The Lord's eagerness to forgive is greater than our capacity to sin.

PRAISE AND THANKSGIVING

When you discover you have long "been had" by a demon, there generally remains the proclivity to continue in the same old rut, even after deliverance has occurred. Such patterns of thought and action were the norm of your life. Even your brain action may have been affected. One way to remove negative effects is to purposely swing the pendulum in the opposite direction by exaggerating your actions and thinking in a new way, until new thinking becomes well established.

Continuing with the example of the spirit of envy, it would be helpful to cultivate a heart of gratitude. Practice saying, "thank you" to God for what He has done for you, and to everyone who gives you anything or does anything for you. Do this until it becomes your automatic response.

When you find yourself being spiritually oppressed, address the attacker face-to-face in personal confrontation. Do not refer to him as an evil force or as a weakness of your own character. Instead call him by name: "Envy, I strike you with the Sword of God. Jesus says you are a liar; that I am delivered out of your hand; I have authority over you. On that authority and through the blood of Jesus I command you to depart!"

The deliverance situation is not like a visible broken leg that has been mended and cannot "return". Rather, it is the person of an evil spirit attempting to once again chain you in bondage. If he is Envy, talk to him as you would to any wicked person. Command him. You are not engaging in a conversation but exercising your superior standing in Christ, demanding he depart from you. The Bible says that after submitting yourself to God, then resist the devil, and he will flee from you (See James 4:7). Keep both points in proper sequence.

We are more vulnerable when weary, tired, sleepy, and physically weak. Make the effort to keep yourself in peak physical condition. Being strong, alert, mentally aware, and emotionally on top enables you to not only recognize subtleties but to be strong enough to resist when he moves against you. Deliverance is spiritual surgery. Intensive care keeps malevolence at bay. Eat the right foods. Take vitamin supplements. Get an adequate amount of sleep. Exercise. Care properly for your body, in which the Lord lives, calling it his temple, keeping his residence clean and orderly (I Corinthians 3:17).

In resisting the devil's approaches, you should examine yourself to see if there is any disobedience that is giving Satan a right to harass. Immediately following a deliverance is the time to be super-alert, doubly on guard. It is good to exaggerate positive behavior during the "post-surgery, intensive care period". Realize that Satan positively will encounter you again. You have the power to do all these things.

MAKING NOTES OF SELF-EXAMINATION

Below is a sample of notes I once wrote about my thoughts and feelings. Writing them helped to diagnose evil spirits at work. Do not imagine there are none, for if you do you are already off track. How do you begin? First priority is to observe the part of you that is hurting, just as a doctor would examine an area of your pain.

Note and date your location. Keep pen and paper handy. This old example is from my time at World Church - Dallas, Texas. Begin writing in full honesty, somewhat as a personal diary, the purpose of which is to discover your spiritual enemy. What is happening that is of concern to you? I was having an uncomfortable feeling that was suspect.

"Whenever I decide it would be wise to make a copy of taped messages for later use at home or office, and glanced at them to make the decision, molded into the fabric of that thought was a negative feeling. Along with the compressing of the original thought came a negative feeling that transitioned so smoothly that it seemed there was no separation between the positive thought and the negative feeling. The feeling is that of gloom, like, 'Don't do It.'" Remember, this was not a thought alone. This was a feeling that occurred alongside a thought.

"Don't do it because of the extra amount of work it would require. It will take you out of your normal pattern of activity. You will have to give up important fellowship and time with your family. This negative feeling is being exerted against the constructive idea."

Then I noted:

"God's thoughts are all positive. Satan's feelings and thoughts are all negative, even though he conceals the treachery. Once I understand this, my choice is either to act in the positive, or else do nothing—which is negative."

I was working in the office during this day and wanted to note that particular feeling so I could determine what (or who) was at work. There were a lot of ministry tape recordings I was making, many for radio broadcast, and I wanted to make an extra copy for my own use. The thought was a desire I had, but with it came an overwhelming heaviness. When I thought of making the duplicates, it became a big chore in my feelings, not my thinking. I knew it would take a lot of time and work. But an inordinate heaviness would clamp down when I thought of doing so. I had recorders set up. Because I was ever alert, I examined my thoughts and feelings. 'Who is that?'" I began to see, and God began to show me this particular conflict is more than it ought to be. I remember the incident very well. It was so subtle, as though it was all one thought and feeling combined.

There was not separation of the two. It was as though a fine, crystal clear, godly thought was implanted, when suddenly the negative gloom swept in. Altogether, the latter influence was, "Don't do it." Satan's weapon of negativity blends so perfectly with our old nature, that discerning its intrusion can be difficult. The two are essentially the same. Be on the alert and watch for his tactics.

"But without faith it is impossible to please him [God]..." (Hebrews 11:6). Writing such things is an action of faith that demonstrates we are fervently seeking Him for truth. God will show you what you need to see. Why? Because your faith is proved by actively seeking it.

Writing is something we can do. We must actually

do something before expecting God to do what we cannot do. He will give us a word of knowledge, reveal hidden things, give revelation. Writing will be effective when done in the mode of "prayer without ceasing". Following the Spirit of God is not so mystical as many believe. He is also known as Common Sense.

As stated earlier, to the degree you are not in control of your body, mind, emotions, or spirit, someone else surely is. If you have tried and been unable to change your mind, attitude, thoughts, habits, or behavior, that is a warning flag waving before you. A proper question to ask is, "If you are not in charge of these faculties, who is?" This is important to discover because each of us is responsible to control our thoughts, words, and deeds and will answer for them. As surely as violation of the natural law of gravity has consequences, so also do violations of spiritual and governmental laws. God ordained them all. It is Satan who is lawless (See I Timothy 1:9).

Understanding of this point will be helped by comparing reality to a Hollywood movie. In the latter, every detail has been repeatedly scrutinized to make sure they are perfectly in accord with the script. Collaborators, designers, artists, and directors make myriad adjustments, even to the ordering of multiple re-takes of scenes to hide flaws of skin, action, fumbled words, wardrobe, and other errors.

When completed, the finished product looks good but is actually a manipulated unreality. Real life is not like that. Humans were designed to be in full control of ourselves without pretense or camouflage.

There was a time when I was steeped in the movie business. Deluded by its fiction, I was later startled and thrilled to learn that sin actually exists, that demons and angels were not just movie-like vocabulary, but are real, animate, intelligent, invisible beings on assignment to influence our lives—angels for good and demons for evil. The latter could even inhabit our body. After gaining a fingerhold, they advance a toehold, a foothold, and finally to a stronghold, through which they often are able to displace normal reasoning, impair cognitive abilities, and disable body functions.

CHAPTER SEVEN

TWENTY TIPS AND TECHNIQUES

A further revelation was that Jesus imparted to his followers both the ability and the command to recognize, overpower, and cast demons out. Important as that is, once expelled they do not die, but lurk nearby to search for a way to reenter. Under certain conditions they do exactly that. Too often we needlessly have given rights to the lawless one to do us damage. Satan's strength is our failure to obey God's commandments, and municipal laws that regulate such as speed limits and stop signs.

These 20 tips are presented to diminish his influence and prevent demonic entrance into your life. I learned them through personal necessity while being tormented for decades. Several will be seen as common sense; others are stipulated by civil law;

some are mandated by Scripture. But all have proved to be effective. Had they earlier been practiced numerous evil spirits would not have found their opening to legally enter into me. Failing to apply them puts us in peril of painful consequences that could otherwise be easily avoided.

The reentry of an evil spirit (demon) usually creates a worse condition than existed before his ouster, because he will return with "seven" other spirits more wicked than himself (See Matthew 12:43-45 and Luke 24-26). Thus, these recommendations are both offensive and defensive. There is no shame in needing deliverance because everyone is born a sinner in need.

Finally, deliverance from one demon does not necessarily mean that all have vacated. Where there is one, most often there are more. Practicing these measures will eliminate the legal ground they rely on to torment their victim. Resistance through repentance (the reversal of unholy thought and conduct) weakens a demon's position and makes deliverance possible, and permanent if maintained. Not all the following applies equally to everyone. But if you are being demoniacally tormented, embracing these strategies will be especially helpful in getting the upper hand and repelling counterattacks that are sure to come.

Pain and torment are powerful motivators that drive us to take strong corrective measures.

Ironically, just considering this subject seriously is itself considered by many to be a desperate measure because most critics do not know the facts. Jesus said, "... forgive them, for they know not what they do." But for those who are knowledgeable, resisting a spiritual enemy is the normal Christian life. Your torments were tailor-made for you by an evil one. Try to recognize them and the specific ground they rely upon, then apply appropriate countermeasures. Claiming the merit of Jesus' blood on your behalf is your primary and super powerful weapon. May you be encouraged to go on the offensive to defend yourself, which destroys the works of the devil at the same time. Then, think of others who may need the help of your ministry. Remember, no one is exempt from the service; we are either warrior or prisoner. Read about it in Second Timothy 3: 1-5 and 4:2-4.

TIP 1: AVOIDING DOUBLE JEOPARDY

There is a righteous law of double jeopardy that protects us. Its effect is that, once full payment for a crime has been made, another payment for the same crime cannot be imposed because that would be illegal. The Lord observe this law while Satan violates it.

Isaiah 53:4-5 reveals that full payment for sin and its effects was made by Jesus Christ on our behalf. That includes every type of moral, mental, physical, and financial failing – including their resulting sickness, pain, disease, and infirmity. Therefore, the punitive effects of a believer's inadvertent sins cannot be legally placed upon those who have repented and been redeemed. We must immediately and ardently resist the satanic onset of double punishment on the basis of this divine law. You qualify for relief each time you repent of a sin, but not before. Our attempts to live righteously are imperfect during earth life. Here, we are being re-conformed, crafted, and restored to the image of Jesus Christ. One may not always be able to fully receive all the benefits of salvation for various reasons, even though none has been rescinded. Our task and privilege is to fervently renounce and resist every negative symptom for which payment has already been made on our account. Personal repentance is often required before a symptom can be alleviated. In First Peter 4:1 we learn "… he that hath suffered in the flesh hath ceased from sin."

Also notice in Luke 13:11-17 that the righteous daughter of Abraham was healed through a direct miracle granted by Jesus, but only after she had for 18 years exhausted all of her money and resources in the effort to defeat the "spirit of infirmity", and not before. This is a proper example for us to follow. First, we should verbally renounce a symptom and the spirit behind it. If the symptom remains, wisdom dictates that we call the church elders and ask for their prayers. It is helpful to also seek authorities or medics. Our first line of defense, however, is to seek the Lord and rebuke the evil spirit in the authority Jesus has given us. More detailed information and instructions are presented in other sections of this book. See James 5:14-15.

TIP 2: NICKNAMES AND NEGATIVE LABELS

An evil spirit can become attached to a name that someone calls you, if the name is allowed to become one's common identity. That name and spirit can also become one's false personality. The result would be a tendency to fulfill the personality of the false name rather than to nurture one's official name and personality. Once inside, the false and malevolent personality would manifest some of the time, but not necessarily all the time. This fact was learned through personal experience.

Many times, during my formative years, my troubled minister father repeatedly railed, "You rotten, hell bound demon! You're not worth a damnable dime!" punctuating it with fearsome treatment. That authoritative declaration loosed demons into my life. Their evil character was acted out from pre-teen years and onward in a destructive manner. Eventually it required multiple deliverances to bring about more normal emotions and conduct. Another outworking of it occurred through a friendly 60-year-old bachelor, a poverty-stricken drunkard neighbor who sexually abused me from the age of nine. Thereafter, he and his gray-haired cohort, the tobacco-chewing, one-legged, beer-brewing Theebe - regularly called me by the name Big Dick instead of using my name. Thirty-two years later, a long-standing, most troublesome demon of that name was cast out of me by minister friends, Frank and Ida Mae Hammond. I am sure the Lord protected the serious Ida Mae from appreciating the humor that crept into my mind as she repeatedly commanded, "that nickname": Come out! Out I say!" Soon enough the spirit departed. She and her husband passed into heaven, after more than a million copies of their excellent book on deliverance, Pigs in the Parlor, were sold.

Consider another example. A man of very short stature was a deacon in his church, in charge of receiving offerings from the congregation. On Sundays he prayed the blessing upon the collection, and without fail, his prayer closed with the words, "And forgive us our shortcomings." Perhaps you can guess the nickname under which he suffered: Shorty. Instead of embracing his design that enabled him to perform special tasks in tight places, the false name became a hurtful curse. If he had asked me for deliverance prayer, I would first have commanded the spirit named Shorty to depart from him. It is probable that this spirit would be the strongman of his life, having been his nickname from childhood. (This illustration is taken from the 1973 book titled, Childhood Vows - The Child within the Man.)

In a similar way, the exercise of useless habits can

draw a demon to the offender. The habitual practice of cracking knuckles, i.e., bending one's fingers until the knuckles pop, permitted a spirit of arthritis to enter into a 17-year-old girl in California. Over time, the continued knuckle popping had permitted the demon to grow so strong that her condition was painfully tormenting by the time she sought help. Medications provided no relief. After I explained the cause and effect of her habit, she promised to stop the cause. The spirit was cast out after admonishing her to resist the temptation to "crack her knuckles". Failure to resist would open the door for that same spirit to re-enter and cause considerably more damage, not only in her fingers, but also to invade other skeletal joints.

Another habit that can be formed during puberty is experimental masturbation. If it becomes habitual it is certain that a demon of that name will enter and make serious trouble. Unless cause and effect are realized, and the offending conduct ceased, there can be lifelong bondage, not only by that spirit, but also by other spirits who would legally enter through the doorway the first leaves open.

The president of an audio Bible production company was of average to short stature. One day he was told by our jovial company auditor, a very large man, "Ralph, you look awfully small in that high-back executive chair!" It was intended to be a cute remark, but instead was hurtful and cut deeply. Within half an hour, Ralph had thrown that expensive high-back chair into a storage shed, and a cheaper, low-back chair was set in its place, in which his small stature was less exposed. Well, known was the fact that this executive was high-strung and defiant with an overbearing "shorty" attitude. He later asked me to pray for his deliverance. The prayer session had limited effect. He was my employer whom I did not want to offend by aggressively criticizing his conduct. The point is, he carried the fear-of-rejection "chip on his shoulder", occasioned by others having mocked his small stature.

Another instance is that of one of my brothers, early in childhood, was viciously and in the worst possible way, called, "Crazy" by our father, which deeply hurt him. Once, when that circumstance was exaggerated, an evil spirit of that character entered, then acted out over the next forty years, negatively affecting the greater part of his life.

Nicknames that we assign to our children can give rise to personality aberrations. Using "Princess" instead of the little darling's true name, may become attached to a spirit of pride, superiority, or haughtiness, for example. The result is an induced feeling of special entitlement which can lead to defiance and an aggressive, "I'll show you!" attitude. Reality ultimately sets in, as it must. Princess would soon learn that she was not a princess at all! Let us realize that life adjustments are already difficult enough without adding the burden of a false personality, via a nickname. It is wise, therefore, to call a person by his or her real name.

TIP 3: CONFESSING SALVATION'S BENEFITS

When our two children were preteens, each time we drove in a car our family of four made a faith profession aloud in unison. It was:

"Praise the Lord! Praise the Lord! Praise the Lord! The blood of Jesus is against you, Satan.

The blood of Jesus is against you, witchcraft. The blood of Jesus is against you, poverty.

Jesus is delivering me now. Jesus is healing me now.

Jesus is prospering me now. Praise the name of the Lord!"

This declaration was foundational to our family's continuing spiritual victory and overall success. Today, the moment I detect mental or physical pain, strain, or sickness, I immediately declare, "Jesus bore my sickness and pain in Pilate's whipping hall (Isaiah 53:4-5). You have no right to this body or soul. Depart now, in Jesus' name!"

A stubborn enemy may require intermittent repetitions of the command until he is defeated.

We must learn to forthrightly declare the facts and benefits of our salvation. Often this is all that a problem requires to be defeated. That said, each of us must use common sense as well. The potential threat of hard pain is that we could become seriously damaged. Medical evaluations still apply.

TIP 4: HUMOR HELPS

Heavy subjects deserve comedy relief. Even brave, warring soldiers laugh and tell jokes between battles.

A lady was being delivered of at least 32 demons over the span of a year. In humor, when about to enter a Denny's restaurant with her, I pulled my young daughter's gray wig from the car, and crookedly stuck it atop my head. Dressed in a suit and tie wearing that goofy wig, I strolled regally beside this lady toward the entrance. Upon seeing it, she literally did a double take and began to laugh uncontrollably. Taking a deep breath, she haltingly asked, "You're not going in there like that are you?" "Why of course", I replied, as we entered the foyer. She stopped, doubled over laughing in genuine heaves so unabashedly and for so long a time that her belly began to hurt!

As we headed toward the booth to be seated, the waitress staff seeing and hearing her belly-laugh, also began to laugh, more because of her laughter than of my strange dress-up. It was infectious! I continued walking with a determined straight face, as though this were my normal appearance. Most certainly that siege of gut-busting laughter seriously aided in her further deliverance over the following weeks. Now separated by two states and two decades, we remain in touch about her marriage, children in college, and for mutual prayer requests.

There is little doubt that when she reads this tip, she will again break into laughter at the remembrance of it, just as I do.

Let us not become too rigid and somber in our religion. It is fun to beat up the devil!

TIP 5: OBEY TRAFFIC LAWS TO AVOID SIN

Often it seems expedient to violate a traffic law. Who isn't in a hurry these days? What is not considered, however, is that such violations are acts of sin that bring punishment under the very laws one has been violating. Scripture warns us not to allow Satan to get an advantage, as seen in 2 Corinthians 2:11. Violation of municipal laws that prohibit speeding, dangerous lane changes, not fastening seat belts, driving with expired license, texting, talking on cell phones, smooching while driving, driving under the influence of drugs or alcohol, and more, are clear evidence of rebellion. Breaking traffic laws gives advantage to the devil to cause crashes (erroneously and unbiblically called accidents) which bring emotional anguish, inconvenience, traffic fines, higher insurance premiums, damage to vehicles and passengers, possible jail time, in addition to a permanent criminal record. Such conduct exhibits a "bad testimony" before others.

Most of this can easily be avoided by obeying municipal and state laws established for our good. The scriptural basis is Titus 3:1: "Put them in mind to be subject to principalities and powers, to obey magistrates, to be ready to every good work." Also, Romans 13:1-6 exhorts: "Let every soul be subject unto the higher powers. For there is no power but of God: the powers that be are ordained of God. Whosoever therefore resisteth the power, resisteth the ordinance of God; and they that resist shall receive to themselves damnation. For rulers are not a terror to good works, but to the evil. Wilt thou then not be afraid of the power? Do that which is good, and thou shalt have praise of the same: For he is the minister of God to thee for good. But if thou do that which is evil, be afraid; for he beareth not the sword in vain: for he is the minister of God, a revenger to execute wrath upon him that doeth evil. Wherefore ye must needs be subject, not only for wrath, but also for conscience's sake. For for this cause pay ye tribute also: for they are God's ministers, attending continually upon this very thing.

In Hebrews 13:17 we are likewise admonished in spiritual matters, "Obey them that have the rule over you, and submit yourselves: for they watch for your souls, as they that must give account, that they may do it with joy, and not with grief: for that is unprofitable for you."

It is well to keep in mind that the devil knows

all the laws and the consequences of violating them. His effort is to cause you to rebel against them, just as he does. If that is not enough incentive to do right, remember, "The wages of sin is death…" (Romans 6: 23).

A note of caution applies: If one in authority becomes corrupt and violates his oath of office, or does wickedly, his delegated authority is thereby negated and must be resisted.

TIP 6: KEEPING DEMONS OUT OF YOUR HOME

Whether new or used personal items, such as clothing, jewelry, furniture, or decorations for your home, many are accompanied by an entity not of God. Such things often are manufactured outside the United States where false gods are worshiped and may well have been dedicated to those gods by their maker or artisan. In such cases, the false god spirit accompanies the items thus dedicated. When brought into your house the spirit attaching to them will wreak havoc on you and your household. That is their assignment.

There are two solutions to prevent such spirits from operating. For spiritually "neutral" items you can verbally take them from the enemy by rededicating them to the Lord. This is done by proclaiming, "Satan, you no longer have any right here. These items are hereby dedicated to the Lord

Jesus Christ as a spoil of war. Depart from them in Jesus' name!"

In the case of idols or demon images, however, they must summarily be removed from your house and renounced: "I renounce you. Depart in Jesus' name." When you do this, their inherent curses also depart with the idol. The best remedy is to destroy the idols and images so that no one else can receive them and their curse (See Deuteronomy 7:25-26).

Among the things in this general category are jewelry boxes, music boxes; stuffed animals, occult books—such as Harry Potter, all things Pokemon, Beanie Babies, dolls and more. Children are vulnerable when they possess toys to which they often assign names, embrace, kiss, and sleep with, as comforting, loving, imaginary personalities.

This principle extends to pets, such as dogs and cats, and more especially to serpents, to which children become physically and emotionally attached to the point of real danger. An example of this danger was exhibited by a man who was seated near my wife and me in Perkins Pancake House. He incessantly meowed loudly while reading his newspaper. Patrons looked around to see if there was a tomcat in the building. He was in some way too involved with a cat. It was comically tragic. I could not see whether he was eating cat food!

Less obvious is the problem of folks who read

pornographic literature or salacious magazine stories that describe crimes and sex acts in spurious settings. Further, photographs of witches, whether of relatives, or others; digital or graphic action video games - fundamentally of violence, mayhem, abuse, and torture. All of these are a magnet that attracts demons. The wise thing is to refrain from their use or viewings or bringing them into your home. But if you are already involved in any of the above, follow the guidelines here and get them out of your house! Then verbally renounce every spirit that came with them.

TIP 7: REMOVING LEGAL GROUND FROM SATAN

"For ye are bought with a price: therefore, glorify God in your body, and in your spirit, which are God's" *(1Corinthians 6:20).*

To repent means to change your mind and conduct from a wrong way to right thinking and living, in accordance with instructions in the Holy Bible. Whatever the Bible embraces or condemns, we must agree to in our thoughts and conduct. This tip focuses on the ever-increasing rebellion in modern society that relates to intimate acts which the Bible condemns. These are presented in the accounts of God's judgment on Sodom and

Gomorrah and elsewhere, such as [Genesis 19: 13, 24-25 and Romans 1:26-28].

The late Bible expositor, Derek Prince was asked, "When is a person forgiven?" He replied, "You are forgiven when you stop doing it." That applies to sins of every description. While one willfully lives in sin, do not imagine that he qualifies for deliverance from the bondage of the very demons who inspire his wrong acts. Repentance in heart, mind, and conduct is required. If one simply cannot quit by the exercise of his own will power, it means he is no longer in charge of that part of his life, and the power of the controlling demon must be broken if there is to be relief. This begins with a change of mind and an active seeking for deliverance. To that end, the body of information in other chapters of this book will guide the seeker.

While it may not be recognized as such, these are acts of rebellion against God. They include habits and practices of cross-dressing; habitual masturbation; oral sex; anal sex; homosexual lifestyle; sex change surgery; carnal bondage using handcuffs, inflicting pain by whips and chains for sensual stimulation; wanton use of hard drugs or cannabis, role reversal of husband and wife, and such like. Objectively, these acts defy common sense. They arise either from ignorance or from open rebellion against God. The primary purpose for reproductive organs is to reproduce offspring "after our own kind" [Genesis

1:24+28]. Aberrations in sexual conduct cannot accomplish this. Thus, their origin is demon inspired and, at best, fulfill unsanitary and unholy desires of the carnal nature. Some Pagan cultures have utterly perished from the earth under judgment by reason of such practices. Notice how seriously the Lord regards such sins: "Rebellion is as the sin of witchcraft and stubbornness is as iniquity and idolatry" (I Samuel 15:23). "Thou shalt not suffer a witch to live" (Exodus 22:18).

Less egregious, but akin to the above, are mutilations of the ear, nose, lips, tongue, belly, and private parts, for the purpose of installing metal rings to impress or satisfy someone. Similarly, cuttings of the body are equally unnatural, though this is done generally out of emotional self-punishment, rather than exhibitionism. Also in this category, is becoming tattooed so profusely as to darken and defile large areas of the body which God owns and designed exactly the way he wants it. While repentance is available, the physical alterations are an enduring testimony of self-indulgence, pride, rebellion, and in some cases, evidence that the offender prefers slavery, as explained in Exodus 21:2-6. Such marks are as long-lasting as a criminal record - essentially permanent. Expressions of self-will (opposing God's will) opens us to demonic invasion. This becomes clear when we read Galatians 5:19-22, which describes the implacable, multi-faceted carnal nature, common to every human. Mutilations of the body are outward expressions of that inward nature.

At a local restaurant, a certain waitress sported "only four tattoos". In answer to my question she replied, "It's habit forming!" Indeed, it becomes much more than that, unless the temptation to be tattooed is resisted. Can you just say, "No"? The remedy to cravings for the unholy is presented throughout this manuscript and proved by Scripture. Be ever mindful that Jesus Christ purchased us from Satan's slavery, at the terrible price of agonizing crucifixion. He made freedom available, but not automatic. "For ye are bought with a price: therefore, glorify God in your body, and in your spirit, which are God's" (1 Corinthians 6:20). When we selfishly deface anyone's property – especially the Lord's – it is an act of vandalism that always carries a penalty.

To remove any curse that goes with rebellious acts such as described here, the offender may repent and pray a simple prayer something like this: "Lord, I am sorry for my sins. I acted in ignorance. Please forgive me. I receive your forgiveness now. Thank you. Amen." Then stop "doing it".

TIP 8: PRINCIPLE OF RETURNING A FAVOR

"And when ye come into a house, salute it. And if the house be worthy, let your peace come upon it: but if it be not worthy let your peace return to you. And whosoever shall not receive you, nor hear your words, when ye depart out of that house or city shake off the dust of your feet. Verily I say unto you, It shall be more tolerable for the land of Sodom and Gomorrah in the day of judgment, than for that city" (Matthew 10:12-15).

Sometimes we suffer negative effects of prayers being prayed by a "Christian" psychic. To help avert that problem we are admonished in Scripture, "And we beseech you, brethren, to know them which labor among you ..." (1 Thessalonians 5:12a & 21). "Prove all things; hold fast that which is good." When malevolent spirits are loosed against us by one who prays for us, it will be helpful to verbally command the spirit to return to its sender. Psalm 109:17-18 and 20 explain the principle thus: "As he loved cursing, so let it come upon him: as he delighted not in blessing, so let it be far from him. As he clothed himself with cursing like as with his garment, so let it come into his bowels like water, and like oil into his bones. Let this be the reward of mine adversaries from the LORD, and of them that speak evil against my soul." Sometimes the individual who has prayed errantly can be identified, but not always. Demons do not "freelance" but are sent on assignment by evil princes who rule from a remote witchcraft center.

In such cases, it will be helpful to verbally command the spirit to depart, and by a factor of ten multiply its fervency to be returned to the sender. Moreover, in the authority given us by Jesus Christ we should loose the Lord's angel to destroy the witchcraft center. This is further explained in chapters two of Book One and chapter six of this book. When that command is given, the original sender will become too busy swatting hornets to continue praying as before. Either way you will be relieved. Most Christian witches are not aware of their spiritual status. That was true in my early life to an exaggerated degree, and the directives above show how the problem was solved.

Outright deceivers will fare much worse than the blissfully ignorant. As for their fate and the Bible's advice on how you should bless them, read all 31 verses of Psalm 109. You will be surprised and relieved. While we are to forgive our human oppressors, the Lord hates their evil works (See Revelation 21:8).

TIP 9: DEFEATING THE MIND-JAMMER SPIRIT

This spirit works by jamming the mind through deception. He makes it to seem that every normal problem and issue must be resolved immediately. Such a compulsion causes undue pressure. The most frequently used lie seems to relate to the payment of bills. That task is usually the most worrisome and stressful because our wellbeing and reputation are at stake. However, the range of subjects is not limited. This demon makes everything seem immediately urgent, though that usually is far from the truth.

This remains a long-standing tactic used by Satan, the "father of lies" (John 8:44).

A roster of urgent problems would include such items as an electrical switch that does not properly operate; the house foundation is shifting; termites are chewing up the walls; dead trees and bushes are causing neighbors to complain; broken boards in your fence are unsightly; your brother is due for a visit and you would be embarrassed for him to see the mess; your real estate investment is being degraded; the bent fender of your car has to be fixed; you need to quickly plan for the funeral of your aged father and invalid mother; your job is in jeopardy; your kids are not doing homework and could be expelled from school; and what about that overdue mortgage payment? The list goes on.

At the base are spirits of fear, anxiety, lies, and false responsibility. Such a jamming of your mind is your signal to stop, think, and recognize your enemy. It is the time to take a deep breath, carefully evaluate the situation, and start writing. Make a list of each "pressing" item by category. First, list the name of your creditors, the dollar amount of their bills, and the actual due date of each. Place them in descending order by due date – soonest to latest. Most of them will have a later, non-urgent date to be paid. In doing so you will discover a few that need to be paid in the full amount; others may be paid as partial payments. In a few instances, a phone call to the creditor will obtain permission to make a partial payment now, and the balance later. Do the same analysis for each category of pressure, which might be unrelated to money – such as multiple human relationships that are uncertain.

Altogether, following this procedure takes away stress by showing that the devil was lying to you all along!

TIP 10: IGNORING VERBAL ENTRAPMENT

Evil spirits use the vocal cords of others to rail against a believer. One of their purposes is to harass; another is to denigrate or cause shame. As an example, a boss I once had walked into my office as many as eight times in one hour. Stern-faced, his glassy eyes darted first to my desk-top, then at me, often without speaking a word. He would pace the floor looking for something to make an accusation or to quarrel about. On the occasions when he spoke, the issues were often without merit, or were repetitions of previous comments. His erratic behavior was clearly irrational and many times, demonic. Sometimes he probed with questions, which, if answered, would violate or entrap me. I was careful. On those occasions my only response was to look straight into his eyes with a spiritually firm, stoic expression, do and say nothing, until he silently turned and walked away.

His restless presence over four years was without peace. One time I obliged when he asked that I pray

LIBERATION OF MIND, WILL, AND INTELLECT

for his deliverance from demonic oppression. After four years we came to a significant spiritual clash. My wife and I determined to move to a new affiliation in Oklahoma and be rid of the oppression.

There were two other occasions when similar baiting occurred in different work environments. One was an egregious, unfounded verbal assault on me by a comptroller in front of the company president! As the accusation concluded, the president, who also was owner, turned and looked at me, waiting for my defense against the charges. My only response was to shake my head in disapproval of the accuser's ignorance, say nothing, then slowly turn in disgust and walk away. The accuser had been seeking a promotion and wanted to impress the president.

A third occasion was in my home. I was telling a true war story to my grandson. During military service on the island of Guam, my best buddy, Corporal David Liggett, had become a machine gunner in the first B-29 Bomber shot down during the Korean War. One crewman was killed while the other eight parachuted over the Pacific Ocean in the dark of night. Their harrowing 30-day survival story is fascinating.

Suddenly, not having seen her standing beside the dining table, the distain-filled voice of my normally loving wife of 52 years blurted, "You're no hero, you just had a desk job! Tell him. Admit it! You worked at a desk. You were no hero. Tell him! Say it! Say it! Why don't you say it?"

I turned to look into her face, somewhat startled at the sudden intrusion, which came totally out of the blue! Instantly I knew a spirit was trying to cause a quarrel between us, sully my reputation in the mind of our grandson, and dishonor my service in the United States Air Force. All Nancy knew about my four years of service that spanned six locations thousands of miles apart, was that I had a blemish-free military record and an honorable discharge, because of which she received veteran's benefits, with more to come. The outburst was abnormal. Me a hero? No, because I am still alive.

Admittedly, in that moment I was tempted to blast her because of her ignorance of all that my service had entailed, all while she was a teenager in grade school. Disgusted, but without comment, I turned back to Riley and continued the story to its conclusion. No heroics had been stated or implied; though I did tell Riley that my buddy, Corporal David Liggett, had been hailed as a hero in his hometown newspaper in Elkins, West Virginia, and that I had twice contacted his mother to give reports on the apparent loss of her son. You may remember that Jesus warned, "A man's foes shall be they of his own household" (Matthew 10:36).

What is clear from these personal examples is that we are not required to reply to a demon who is looking through the eyes and speaking through vocal cords of his victim, whether it is your boss, spouse, or friend.

Two biblical examples also apply. One is Matthew 27:13-14, when Roman Governor Pontius Pilate questioned Jesus, under threat of death. "And he [Jesus] answered him to never a word; insomuch that the governor marveled greatly." Another is Acts 16:16-18, when a spirit of divination in a demonized woman repeatedly taunted Apostle Paul over many days. The apostle did not respond or react in any way. Finally grieved, he abruptly turned and commanded the demon to come out of the woman. The demon fled. A believer should choose the time, place, and circumstance as to when and how to respond to a demon. It is inappropriate for a calculating evil spirit to decide, and in so doing ensnare the believer. For clarification and context about my wife's comments above, we had a highly productive, loving, and faithful marriage of 52 years. We both knew our marriage had been divinely arranged, needful of each other in ministry. Sometimes we were like sports opponents - abrasive but entertaining!

An additional major point is to be made. On one occasion she blurted out, "I'm sick of deliverance!", at a time when I really needed her help in a deliverance meeting. She opted out. That was a highly consequential misjudgment on her part because the Lord thereafter withheld her further deliverance from an evil spirit that plagued her, named Man-hate. Admittedly it became a devil of a problem from time to time, but we both had rough edges that needed to be worn off, and, as "iron sharpens iron" by abrasion, we were both helped in that way.

Wisdom is to never refuse deliverance when the Lord makes it available to you, as it could well be the very last offer to come your way. "Seek ye the Lord while he may be found, call ye upon him while he is near" (Isaiah 55:6). Today is the day of salvation. To let a demon speak through you is a serious mistake. Even so, when it occurs, the offended believer does not have to speak or react in reply. Obviously, however, when such a mistake is made, mutual forgiveness must be initiated to bring healing in the relationship.

TIP 11: DEFEATING DEMONIC SETUPS

Demons work by plan. They make setups to move you into their trap. One trick is to cause several frustrations in a row, perhaps five in one morning. The purpose is to disrupt or lock up our mind to cause delays and emotional distress, especially when an important matter is being worked on. Through one such frustrating experience I learned a simple technique that defeated their plan. When frustrations quickly pile up, if you will purposely stop all activity, shut off your thoughts, lie down and sleep for 10 minutes, their setup will be defeated. Why? Because their trap requires you to be awake and busily using your mind. If your mind shuts off a few minutes, their power is shut off and the stress they were setting up is broken. They will have lost the battle and must start again from ground zero. Therapists know the benefit of taking a short nap but do not know this spiffy spiritual part of it.

Here is how it works. Once I was using an automatic typewriter that relied on a bank of electrical relays – a Flexowriter. Sometimes the keyboard would lock up. When that happened, all I had to do was flip off the power switch. Without the power to energize them, the relays would immediately reset to zero. A moment later I flipped the power switch back on and everything that had been locked was released to work perfectly. That was the clue! A spirit of Ohm causes trouble in electronics. Ohm is a measure of electricity that can somehow be manipulated. Often God lets us see invisible realities through our understanding of things that are visible. This principle is shown in Romans 1:20. "For the invisible things of him [God] are clearly seen, being understood by the things that are made…". The Flexowriter I used, was one of the things made, so the principle, once revealed, obviously had to work. The underlying problem in the visible realm was understood by seeing it from God's point of view, relating it to a function of invisible electricity. It is helpful to remember that everything that is now visible originated in the unseen realm.

TIP 12: DEMONIC RESISTANCE TO MEDICATION

Webster's Dictionary defines "Immunize" as simply: "To make immune." Medical doctors immunize patients against various types of viruses such as influenza, diphtheria, pneumonia, and the like. Generally, immunizations help to protect us. While this is well known, the society of invisible persons and their workings and activities are less known. There is an undefinable connecting place where an evil spirit meets with our soul and body to cause a variety of conflicts. The result of that meeting is observable in our afflicted body, mind, and emotions. In a real sense, demons act similarly to the various viruses that attack us; indeed, they can directly or indirectly either cause or simulate them. No matter what natural measures are taken, we must also steadfastly take our stand against the devil and his demons on a spiritual warfare basis (See Ephesians 6:11-17). This does not rule out the exercise of common sense in seeking needful medical advice from those who know more than we do about a malady, and medicines that bring relief.

A medical doctor may prescribe an approved medicine to treat a physical symptom. Depending upon the degree of its effectiveness, its dosage might be increased, or another medication introduced to work in concert with the first. He will make dosage adjustments over time until treatment becomes more effective. Often, when a palliative cream is applied to one's skin to relieve a sore spot, it works in part. Even when the problem or pain is caused or exacerbated by a demon, some medications may bring temporary relief. An extreme problem would be a migraine headache. Whenever it is caused by an indwelling demon, which it often has been, no cure is possible with medications because the demon remains there to perpetuate the torment until he is cast out. I have personally applied that deliverance remedy on behalf of others with astonishing, instantaneous, and permanent relief. No evil spirit can immunize himself from the power of God that is authoritatively applied against him. However, an evil spirit can sometimes work around an issue and may develop resistance to a particular medication that had been used with positive effect. Often an evil spirit can generate a skin malady to incur torment. These include small bumps that develop into skin cancer, psoriasis, itching, and much more. Our immediate natural impulse is to find a medication to alleviate the irritation. I refer primarily to non-fatal or less advanced diseases. I do not know very much about how the invisible "medical demons" work, only that they often induce irritation of skin, scalp, and other parts of the body. Often times they induce a sudden sharp pain without a legitimate cause. I have repeatedly been thus victimized over the decades but have learned how to diminish or destroy their set-ups. One helpful action has been to alternate from one medication to another, both designed to relieve the same symptom, but having different formulations of ingredients. Best relief seems to require a rotation of three medications, each for a short period of time. I know this sounds a bit odd, but what part of this subject does not? It seems that individual ingredients within a formulation are targeted by our adversary, and a seemingly modest change from those exact ingredients requires the evil one to start over in his effort to bypass your immunity.

Looking a little further, there appears to be a connection between our bodies having been created from elements of earth [Genesis 1:11], and certain ingredients in medications also originating in the earth and its vegetation [Genesis 2:7-9]. There is a further reference to tree leaves being a healing agent [Revelation 22:2].

Realize also that, because demons do not die, they have accumulated an incalculable amount of knowledge about human bodies and souls over thousands of years. In contrast, each human lives through only one short life span generation. For example, have you ever read in your newspaper the obituary for a demon? No, because they do not die. But thousands of obituaries are printed daily for humans who have died within "a few short years".

This means that demons have learned how, and have perfected ways to torment us, of which mortal humans are still trying to discover.

Most of our learning comes through personal trial and error and through other humans who likewise shall die within seven or eight decades. The idea here is to find and do whatever works to eliminate torment, because at best we already have enough to deal with every day.

We work better when we feel good. If your medication has "lost" its effectiveness, why not try another to treat the same problem. It has worked for me. Consider that medics continue to develop effective "generic" drug substitutes to replace an original formula that worked well for a while. What this shows is that a variety of earth elements can be formulated in different mixes to treat the same malady. Knowing that demons are always involved in our lives, perhaps this suggestion may lead you to more relief.

TIP 13: EXERCISING THE MIND OF CHRIST

It is only believing Christians who can exercise the mind of Christ. If you are a believer, the Holy Spirit guides your thoughts in the ways of integrity. This is not true for atheists. As optimists, we tend to believe that those we do business with will not lie but will keep their commitments. That sometimes happens. But too often their neglect causes us trouble, wastes our time, and causes frustration.

A better alternative is to assume in advance that the other party to your transaction is blind to godly integrity, is selfishly motivated, or worse. Under this assumption, when a commitment is made by another, we are wise to expedite it by making follow-up phone calls.

Efficiency is achieved when we follow three steps.

1. The department manager just now said to you, "Yes," he will make the exchange. He will be available inside the store, day after tomorrow from noon to 3:00 pm. This is a propitious moment to ask for his business card. Have him write "Even Exchange on Model WF-7620 Epson Printer upon return of the old one".

2. On the day appointed for the transaction, again call their office before packing up your old printer and driving to the store. Confirm with the clerk by telephone that they now have the printer WF-7620 in stock and will hold it for one hour for you. Also confirm that the store manager is present, and he will be there for the next hour. When these issues are affirmed you can proceed with relative confidence that the exchange will be made as promised. Negative or inconclusive answers would help you decide the next steps.

3. Once your transaction is successful and

complete, be sure to thank the clerk and the store manager for their excellent service and tell them you will not only be back but will also recommend others to their store! Remember, those who serve us are often verbally abused by customers. Shaking their hand and saying "Thank you" is always a blessing to them.

Make expeditious follow-up calls like these a matter of personal policy in your business life. Doing so will prevent a waste of time, make you more efficient, and preserve your peace of mind. The idea is: Trust but verify. It seems to usually require three follow-up calls from the comfort of your home or office to keep things going your way. But that is a lot better than spending three hours, making three trips, and still getting the runaround by three different, indecisive clerks.

The longer you exercise this policy, the more time you will save, and your employer will soon recognize your excellent efficiency and reward you appropriately.

TIP 14: PREVENTING DROWSINESS

Look beyond the obvious here because this deals more with demonic activity than with a physical condition. Every driver knows that drowsiness can be deadly when driving and be especially problematic on long trips. It typically develops when your body has been drained of energy or when you simply have not had proper rest.

Having driven about two million miles and been fatigued many times, I had to find things that would keep me awake when driving long distances alone. Drinking coffee was not enough. The breakfast meal was effective the first two hours, but its supply of energy soon ran out. Before departing, the prepared sandwiches, fruit, munchies, and soft drinks to eat along the way would be helpful. However, this did not always prevent drowsiness. The dilemma, then, was to consider not only the physical, but also potential spiritual causes of drowsiness. Knowing that Satan's objectives are to "steal, kill, and destroy", what better way than to cause a driver to fall asleep while driving at highway speeds and crash head-on into another vehicle? Such demonic intrusions nearly always involve fatalities.

As adversary warriors, the question to keep in mind is, "What would I do if I were in the enemy's shoes?" One of us is invisible and never sleeps, which brings us to the germane aspect of the problem. In the natural, drowsiness appears to be caused by low energy or exhaustion, but often it is not. Rather, it can be the deceptive, coerced, and oftentimes overpowering manifestation of a demon. Either way, the automatic result is to nod the head and fall sleep.

My problem was typical. Preparation for a trip included a good night's sleep, a box of food stuff and drinks to bolster energy. In spite of that, quite often my eyes would become irresistibly closed to the point of sleep, as if from exhaustion. Pulling off the highway, I would sleep about 15 minutes before proceeding somewhat refreshed. But the same level of drowsiness soon returned. Puzzled as to the cause, I would drive to the next roadside rest area. There I refreshed myself with a walk, a drink of water, and a visit to the men's room. Let me not be indelicate here: my restroom visit included the sit-down type for a man, which brought relief. It was immediately noticeable that such a refreshing brought instant help from the unwarranted, forced sleepiness. Soon I discovered the connection and determined that repeating the same type of rest stops would be a part of my battle plan.

In deliverance ministry, I noticed on several occasions the candidates' complaint included constipation of the bowels backed up for days. In extreme cases it would be for weeks, and in two cases, more than a month. To solve that problem, a demon was forcibly expelled, which resulted in the candidates substantial and urgent emptying in the nearest restroom, and sometimes before that! The individuals were both amazed and pleased to learn of this unrecognized solution to their problem.

My conclusion is that demons [Jesus referred to them as "unclean spirits"] in some way feed, not only on juices in the blood, but also draw strength from excrement that remains in the body. (See War on the Saints, by Jesse Penn Lewis, page 266 for a similar testimony.) There was one egregious case in a southwestern state where a husband and wife actually, and mutually, ingested each others' dung during their intimate relations – believing their warp was an expression of love for each other. It was easy to discern the demonic influence in that relationship. The man claimed to be a Christian and to have written a book on salvation.

From a purely medical perspective, doctors advise patients to evacuate their bowels once a day, knowing from experience that, when excrement remains inside more than a few days it could generate disease. Their advice, while sound, is without benefit of the spiritual insight discussed here. As so often occurs, doctors treat symptoms with traditional medical protocols, but are not trained to consider the less obvious spiritual causes and remedies explained in the Holy Bible.

We learn from Scripture and practice that the body and mind are literal battlefields of opposing invisible forces. That fact is the main thrust of this discussion. Doctors assign names to symptoms and prescribe remedial medications to the best of their knowledge. While this often brings some relief, these wonderful people can go no further. It is the Lord who does the healing and gives revelation.

Another example of falling asleep while driving was that of my 17-year-old grandson. Within two weeks of obtaining his driver's license, he had two crashes—one the very day his license was issued! He fell asleep driving on his daily four-mile errand. A doctor prescribed a medicine to treat the condition called narcolepsy. Webster's Dictionary defines narcolepsy as "a condition characterized by brief attacks of overwhelming drowsiness or deep sleep." Aw shucks! I must have had that condition over 50 years! Except that mine was immediately cured when Derek Prince cast the spirit of slumber out of me (Romans 11:8). Notice also that Jesus cast out an evil spirit called Epilepsy—not so different from Narcolepsy. The lesson is that we must employ the appropriate remedy for both the physical and the spiritual causes of drowsiness. The best preventive policy is to use the bathroom remedy daily. Your doctor will agree with that assessment, if only for "traditional" reasons.

TIP 15: MOOD CHANGERS

When your mood is sad or morose because of any variety of circumstances, there are several positive things you can do to convert it into joy:

- Go out to a restaurant. Look at a small family eating pancakes. Walk over and compliment the cute little girl on her excellent work in coloring the place mat, for staying within the lines. Pull out your quarters and place them into her chubby hand as a reward for doing a good job. See how delighted she becomes, turning to coyly show them to mommy.

Almost in tears, mommy tells her, "It's okay. Now what do you say to the nice man?" "Fank you." You will see the most genuine, wonderful smiles of gratitude for complimenting her child. If it's a boy, however, you'll get his "high five" hand slap, and a stoic nod from his proud daddy. I ask you, "What could be better than that?" What a joy it is to encourage the only remaining innocents on earth. "Of such is the Kingdom of Heaven". I have thus been blessed dozens of times.

- Write an overdue note of kindness or praise to someone deserving and mail it.
- Ask an elderly widow if you may cut the overgrown brush, weeds, and saplings to dress up her yard. One time 35 years ago, I did this, and her response was so deeply humbling and unforgettable that it still touches my heart. She blurted out, "You're from God." That was her way of saying yes, and nothing more, in tears of gratitude. She was widowed, crippled, and had lived alone 52 years. How this sweet Emily must have ached for such an expression of kindness from someone, anyone, even a stranger. Her blessed remark so humbled and motivated me that I hired a man who, together with my young son, John, and myself worked two weeks at the task. Thus, together we share in lifelong blessing. Neighbors took

notice and some thanked us, as it helped the neighborhood as well.

- Buy yourself a one-hour back massage to feel refreshed and rejuvenated.
- Switch tasks for a little while and do some little thing altogether different from the present drudge – something that will give you an easy victory. Even a little victory will give you a big boost in morale.
- If angry, engage yourself in strenuous activity for an hour to work off steam and diffuse pressures; go ride a bike, swim, play hard. Use anger as fuel to do good. It refreshes your body and soul.
- Listen to some godly comforting music. It will lift your spirit and drive away evil spirits. Sing along, too, even if you sound like an old crow. It works like an insect repellent. See an example of this in 1 Samuel 16:23.

Any of these mood changers can reset your mood and increase productivity. Remember that God does not work instead of us, but with us.

- Stop a moment to consider all your blessings. Tell God how grateful you are for everything he has done for you. You may be amazed at how quickly these things turn your mood from sadness to joy.

TIP 16: DEFEATING ENEMY TACTICS

If your propensities include the problem of rage and anger as mine had, here is a technique I have used to great advantage. Employing it could prevent an angry outburst that might ruin your attitude for a day, week, or longer. Anticipate the possibility that a party whom you want to "ask for a favor" might say, "No," which would normally infuriate you. Do this: Say aloud to yourself in advance, "I know what could happen here, and if it does, I will accept it as God's will. I will not become upset or get angry." At the very least it will bring a smile to your face because you will have defeated your anger enemy before he could strike. When you have done this a few times it will become a way of life. It puts you in control instead of being caught off guard by a surprise attack. It is as simple as making the decision in advance to preemptively respond to rejection in a positive way.

There is a related principle in Scripture: "Seek him [the Lord] while he may be found" (Isaiah 55:6). Sad to say, in my own family, on the matter of seeking knowledge (especially of deliverance from evil spirits) some relatives waited too long. The consequence was a painful, compromised existence and shortened life of misery for two of them. This does not suggest they were lost from salvation of the soul, but it was very far from the "life more abundantly" promised in John 10:10. Too often it was their direct refusal to believe that Christians could have a demon dwelling within their body, leaving them victimized by that lie. It should be obvious that, as a person grows old, the body and mind do not grow stronger but ultimately weaker. The fact that a demon is left unchallenged lets him grow stronger and overtake a weakening mind and body. Confirmation of this fact is seen when visiting a few nursing homes to see and smell the glaring examples. Obviously, residents of such places are there because of any variety of causes and conditions too diverse to name.

Most of us know someone who has said something like, "The cancer grew without us knowing. By the time it was discovered it was too late. Now it's not treatable and we've been told it will be fatal. Had we known it was there, her life could have been saved." So it is with demonic entities.

Knowledge is power. Demons can be defeated and evicted by scriptural resistance. "Submit yourselves therefore to God. Resist the devil, and he will flee from you" (James 4:7). When false doctrine or pride prevails, the devil wins. But if you obey Ephesians 6, you will prevail and live-in victory. It is a way of life, not a single event. "Put on the whole armor of God" as a way of life (Ephesians 6:11).

Here is an example of overturning a problem by simply making a decision. I spend a lot of time in restaurants. A few waitresses were making mistakes while dispensing meals, spilling water, dropping utensils, and more. They apologized, "I don't know what's the matter with me today; I'm so nervous." Loving them, I explained that if they would slow down, be deliberate and control every movement through concentration, their problems would be solved, and they would be more efficient. They followed the advice and thanked me for the good result. The mistakes ceased. This is true in both the natural and spiritual realms.

When serving in the United States Air Force in Guam, I owned a 1942 military Jeep. Driving off-road up a mountainside, the engine would nearly stall unless I slowed by shifting the transmission into granny-low gear and engaging the four-wheel drive, the most efficient to overcome gravity. I was amazed at the rugged ability the Jeep had to wonderfully scale difficult terrain in that mode. That example applies not only for vehicles, but also for us to overcome spiritual obstacles. Slow down. Set your mind in granny-low and be very deliberate. You will be amazed at the results.

TIP 17: REPENT OF LONG-STANDING LIES

It has been said that the mere motive of a Christian is a loud proclamation to God in heaven. I give you my fresh testimony today of that fact. For over two weeks a vertebra in my upper spine gave me a sharp pain that immobilized my upper body when I moved in a certain way. As my efforts to make a spinal adjustment failed, I went to see a chiropractor for help. For three days in a row his best efforts did not fix the problem. Finally, I regarded its cause as more spiritual than physical. A problem of any nature may be caused by sin, including mine. Looking for any unresolved sin in my life, I asked the Lord to show it to me.

Instantly the name Neal appeared in my mind. Then I remembered I had promised Neal Nain that I would send him an autographed book when the manuscript was published. Only one time I tried to contact him by e-mail three years later, which apparently did not reach him. He had moved out of Oklahoma to a university that offered a doctorate degree and scholarship in physics. My promise had been definite, and the book was published but had not been sent. That means I had lied to him – a terrible Christian witness.

What I now understood was that making a false promise is an egregious sin. Revelation 21:8 explains that a lie is regarded by God as equal to murder. God remembers. He is supremely emotional about the conduct of his children – very jealous (Ex. 20:5 and 34:14, Nahum 1:2). Whom He loves, He chastens (Hebrews 12:6-7). Lies told to me by others had caused loss, disappointment, anger, damage to my publishing work, broken relationships, and so much more. Like God, we also hate lying. Why? Because whenever one of his children tells a lie, it negatively affects Him, his reputation, and kingdom, fully as much as a lie affects me personally. As Derek Prince once stated, "Jesus is a jealous lover." That is a remarkable fact.

My immediate response was to repent by fulfilling the promise to send the book. I wrote Neal's name – along with a few others to whom I had half-committed to send the book. Now here's the salient connection. The moment I made the commitment afresh to keep the promise, the Lord knew he could depend upon me to obey. Therefore, the painful spinal vertebrae condition was instantly alleviated with four connected sneezes in deliverance! The demon's stronghold was broken.

I am extremely impressed with sure knowledge that God intimately experiences our emotions and pains [Hebrews 4:15-16]. We need to just be honest, realizing we are "on camera" every moment of our lives. Our repentance brings immediate comfort to God and to ourselves as his children, made to "...sit together with Him in heavenly places in Christ Jesus" (Ephesians 2:6). What could be more intimate than that? My tip to you by way of this testimony, is that you make your life much better by repenting of any sin the Lord reveals to you, be it ever so small in your eyes.

TIP 18: MAKE RESTITUTION NOW

At first, I wrote of another minister who had failed to make restitution where it seemed to be needed. Then the Lord prompted me: "touch not mine anointed and do my prophets no harm" (I Chron. 16:22). Therefore, I edited the reference to him. Instead of pointing to another, I was prompted to use my personal sin as the example. How like our old nature to "blame" someone else for doing a wrong of which we also are guilty! The war goes on.

A person serving time in prison for committing a crime does not constitute restitution to anyone who was damaged by his crime. These are separate matters, one of an earthly court and the other a God matter. Even when the offended person(s) say they forgive you for having done the deed, that also is not restitution to them. Further, when the Lord Jesus forgave you, His payment of your debt was not you making restitution for the damage you caused to His kingdom. Forgiveness is one thing, restitution is another. Jesus served your prison term to satisfy the sentence the Judge imposed for your crime. Now the Lord awaits you making restitution.

You may ask "What, then, is restitution?" Using an event of my life to answer, when I was a younger teenager, I associated with an unsavory 17-year-old neighbor named Ted. Together we ended up setting a car on fire to help cover another sin. The explosion of the gas tank was big, which we heard while escaping out of town along the railroad tracks.

Confused about salvation in those years, I had not fully repented. My way of ultimately doing that was to give automobiles to several people in need. Included were one Mercury station wagon; three Cadillacs; one Ford sedan; two Buick sedans, one Lincoln town car; and one other vehicle. It is proper to make things right where possible.

It was about 33 years after my angry abuses that the Lord appropriately reminded me of certain unresolved details. That set me on a course of making restitutions whenever there was opportunity to do so. By the time I got around to contacting some whom I had wronged, both they and their families had passed away.

One time, however, I did admit to a wrong that resulted in me being three weeks in a trial court involving a man's twenty-five-million-dollar lawsuit. I had lied to receive a $50,000 bribe which, at the time was equal to 10 years of my salary. The Lord spared me being charged with a crime. In that case, my restitution was to give public testimony of personal guilt which exonerated the innocent parties and forfeited the $50,000 bribe money. My conscience was thereby cleared before man and God.

Here is another example of the need for a man to make restitution. My late brother, Philip Mark Keklikian, and I often laughed upon its remembrance. It may seem less significant than the foregoing, yet it serves to emphasize a point.

In our 30's, a Mr. Hickumbothum, decades

earlier, had made some kind of deal with our dad, Tony Abraham Keklikian, known as "Brother Tony". Twenty years later Mr. Hickumbothum died, and I informed Dad of his death. His only response was a matter of fact, "Owed me a nickel".

Do you see the point? Dad merely stated the fact that had for twenty years remained foremost in his memory of the life of Mr. Hickumbothum. Whatever good the man might have done was less memorable than that one 5-cent sin! How typical! Heaven's books contain the record of all such events. "Small" offenses and breaches of integrity pile up. It is wise to keep our promises. "So then, every one of us shall give account of himself to God" (Romans 14:12). Putting off the old nature is like slowly dying from a "thousand small cuts".

In my opinion it is compromised Christianity that will not make restitutions where possible. Notice in Luke 19:2-9 that the rich little man in a tree in Jericho, named Zacchaeus, said to Jesus, "…if I have taken anything from any man by false accusation, I restore him four-fold." And Jesus replied, "This day is salvation come to this house…". What day was that? It was the day restitution was made. Are you willing to examine yourself in this regard?

TIP 19: THE ROLE OF MUSIC IN DELIVERANCE

All forms of music stimulate, attract, or convey spirits in an undefined way, whether good or evil.

Worldly music – acid rock, hip hop, "long hair" classical, voodoo drumbeats, and the like, usually do not glorify God. In general, they tend to draw or strengthen worldly spirits and inspire "dirty dancing", provocative physical gyrations with mob screaming as expressions of human emotions.

The opposite type of music glorifies God in lyrics, tenor, and tempo, especially when sung or performed in anointed worship with an effort toward excellence, thereby pleasing the Holy Spirit.

I Samuel 16:14-23 supports this view. After the Lord anointed David to be King, we see several wonderful results of such music. King Saul was being vexed by an evil spirit. His servants were ordered to seek out a man, "…a cunning player on the harp."

v. 23 And it came to pass, when the evil spirit from God was upon Saul, that David took an harp, and played with his hand: so Saul was refreshed, and was well, and the evil spirit departed from him. "

Few among us could be described as being like David – an expert musician, writer of Psalms, mighty and valiant man of war, prudent, handsome, and most importantly, "The Lord was with him." Certainly, these are kingly virtues. The main point however, is that godly music drives away evil spirits.

My advice to a lady who was struggling to defeat her bondage to deadly nicotine was to play godly music and sing the lyrics as well. Whether driving a vehicle or busy at home, this form of worship\warfare is easy and will be effective against any demonic stronghold. Persisting in it will make you the winner in your struggle to be free of such bondage. Some falsely believe that cigarette smoking is not a sin. It has proven to be destructive to the human body. Scripture says, 1. Your body is a temple of the Holy Spirit; and 2. God will destroy anyone who destroys His temple. This is fair warning (see I Corinthians 3:16-17).

TIP 20: THE POWER OF THE LORD'S PRAYER

If you read, "the Lord's Prayer" (Matthew 6:9-13) every day, you would soon memorize it. It takes two minutes to pray the words. From memory thereafter, you would be able to pray it anytime of day or night. Your sleep will be better, you will have peace in your mind and heart, knowing you are assured of your place in Paradise – just a little while ahead.

Its power will protect and deliver you from "the evil one". It will heal your hurts and give you special standing with God, as praying it is obedience to His Son's directive. You will find that, indeed, you have a Father – the best One possible. He is both in heaven and on earth, and inside you as well. Make this a habit so exercised that its provisions will never leave your thinking or trust. Adding the 23rd Psalm will double the benefit.

DAVID KEKLIKIAN

WARFARE DECREE

"...decree a thing and it shall be established." Job 22:28

The following decree proved to be effective in turning a near disaster into a blessing. It had come through intense frustration from a truly demonized tenant family who were severely damaging our rental property 700 miles away. The lady, with two small and inordinately beautiful children, was intermittently living in adultery with an unrelated married man, who also gave her money. Illegal drugs were involved in the whoredom as well. No husband was to be found.

Angry with the devil, I sought the Lord for an answer. This decree is what He gave me. I wrote it on paper before driving to Houston, confronting the family, then declaring this warfare decree while walking through the premises.

When all the rooms had been thus cleansed, I placed the document in the attic where it would be a permanent testimony. Thereafter, from anywhere in the world I could confidently remind the Lord of its presence and ask that He dispatch a warring angel to enforce its provisions. This gave me wonderful assurance. The result was so positive that I repeated placing the Decree in other properties. Every one of them became very profitable investments.

Demons who remain in a property vacated by previous tenants are called "Squatter Spirits." This term is borrowed from a history book that describes folks who, though not authorized, secretly took refuge in a vacant property, and acted as though they were the owners.

A word of caution is needful: This decree works only for believers in Jesus Christ. I advise against its use by non-believers, lest a negative effect occur. Read about such a happening in Acts 19:13-16.

This decree is to be declared aloud in a commanding voice while walking through each room of the property. When the declaration has been completed, place the printed decree in a secure part of the property. My placement is usually in the attic.

DECREE FOR HOUSE AND FAMILY

Our Father and our God, we thank you that we

who have asked your Son Jesus Christ to save our souls have the privilege of coming boldly before you, just as a child may boldly come to his parent. We believe the Holy Bible to be your true Word. In 1 Chronicles 29:11 and 13, You tell us that You have the greatness, power, glory, victory, and majesty: and all that is in heaven and in earth is yours. It is your Kingdom, O Lord, and you are exalted as head above all. Now therefore, our God, we thank you and praise your glorious name."

You also say in Luke 10:19-20. "Behold, I give unto you power to tread on (evil spirits called) serpents and scorpions, and over all the power of the enemy; and nothing shall by any means hurt you."

Therefore, to carry out this authority on behalf of the Kingdom of God, and in agreement with these witnesses, it is hereby decreed that:

This property, known as our household—inside and outside, land, buildings, inhabitants, and animals—are now taken from the satanic spiritual enemy as a spoil of war, and that these are hereby dedicated to the Lord Jesus Christ. This place is set apart and made holy by our testimony, through the Blood of Jesus Christ. From today forward, all persons in full agreement with this spiritual decree shall be blessed in accordance with this decree.

IT IS FURTHER DECREED:

That through this act of dedication, every evil

spirit present, whether named or not named, must bow to Divine authority, and must now vacate these premises, and depart from its owners and tenants, by order of the Lord Jesus Christ, through us.

We break every curse brought by previous occupants, every curse from antiquity against property and family, whether inherited generational curse, whether upon family through addictions, poverty, disease, deformity, the occult, or by iniquity. We tell you that Jesus Christ took all curse upon Himself on the Cross for us. Therefore, all curses are hereby returned upon those who placed them.

As you have no rights, neither part nor lot in this matter—and no ability to resist—you will obey us, as we are the redeemed of the Lord. There is no salvation for you evil spirits; you will be forever cast into hell by the Lord Jesus Christ.

NOW, Satan, we address you directly:

We call forth all foul spirits not of God—spirits that cause property damage, blight, disease, and death; pest and pestilence; clutter and junk; neglect and intrusion, worry, fear, theft, want, and insufficiency: We command you to desist and expire in your works of darkness.

You unclean spirits of Poverty, Pornography, Rape, Incest, Sexual Uncleanness, Evil Imaginations, Lasciviousness, Adultery, Lust and Lust of the Eyes; spirits of Battery, Child Abuse, Shame, and

Worry. We hereby command you to vacate these premises, its owners and occupants. You demon forces of Rebellion, Rejection, Unforgiveness, Hate, Anger, Violence, Misery, Murder, and Retaliation, Nicotine, Drunkenness; Drug Addiction, Lying and Deception; Spirits of Occult: Ouija, Witchcraft; False Religions; and all kindred spirits.

Uproot yourselves now as we come against you through the blood of Jesus Christ, by the anointing of the Holy Spirit, on the authority of the Word of God.

You are ordered to abate, expire and desist your operations in this property, its owners and occupants, including animals.

DECREE FOR OUR NATION

We further decree that Satan's forces must now roll back from our municipal and national leaders; and that 100,000 antichrist centers of witchcraft be destroyed by their pronounced curses being returned upon their own heads. Let the proud who deceive the public be snared and put to shame according to their own lying words.

This shall apply in the metropolitan locations of our town, and of Washington, D.C.; New York, NY; Philadelphia, PA; Chicago, IL; Houston-Dallas, TX; San Diego, Los Angeles, San Francisco, Sacramento, CA; Seattle, WA; Portland, OR, along the borders of our nation, and its environs.

We now implore you, our God, to loose holy angels to engage in this battle on behalf of the Kingdom of God, on the basis of Hebrews 1:14, Matthew 18:19, and Mark 16:17-18.

Having made this proclamation before Almighty God in the presence of witnesses, as it is written, so let it be done, in the mighty name of Jesus. Amen.

INTERVIEW QUESTIONS AND ANSWERS

1. Tell me about your book. What is it about?

Answer: Book One was the first of three that reveal the ongoing warfare between the invisible forces of God and of Satan. They explain its cause and purpose from man's beginning until now, which is to settle their dispute over freeing enslaved humanity. One of the more important revelations is that the demonic kingdom is operated as a worldwide governmental hierarchy. Ruling spirits compel lesser demons to stalk righteous humans from place to place and report back for further orders. They are instructed to find a way to enter into humans, torment, and kill them.

Typical battles are here exemplified in eleven cases of deliverance from demons which I personally ministered. Two other cases are in extreme detail of demons and the minister battling each other, one demon speaking in the two languages of Swahili and English. Each case is both testimonial and a resource through which teachers may encourage others to engage their enemy and win their personal battles.

2. I have to admit that sounds pretty far-fetched.

Answer: Indeed, it does!

3. Do you find that people actually believe there literally are – as you say – invisible agents of evil?

Answer: Many do, others do not. But everybody agrees that bad things occur to cause pain, anguish, and death. Jails, hospitals and graveyards are full to overflowing with victims who could not answer why their calamity happened to them. Newscasters report all the bad stuff but cannot tell us the reason for it, even questioning what motivated the perpetrators.

4. Are you convinced that the answers you provide are legitimate?

Answer: The first 37 years of my life were devoid of answers to misery. Over the next 50 years, however, answers came progressively as tormentor demons were cast out of me. That revelation changed my life so dramatically that I pursued it with zeal. In a similar way I have been able to help others. There are multiple surface causes of calamity, but the origin of all of it is the same.

Evil is not a mere principle but is the unalterable expression of Satan, the devil. Jesus said that we should pray, "...deliver us from the evil one" [Luke 11:4].

5. How did your personal help come about?

Answer: When a medical doctor, a psychologist, and psychiatrist were unable to help, I finally turned to the Holy Bible to find an answer. Since I didn't have one to read, I stole one out of a motel room in Michigan and read it avidly for two years. I was astonished to learn that Jesus could actually raise the dead! I couldn't get away from it. I found that only He could solve my problems. Since that time, my study of the Scripture has been the basis and rationale for the way I have lived and for writing these books.

6. If someone owns a Holy Bible to read, why would they need or want your book?

Answer: Obviously, the Bible is the primary source for everyone. But it is so comprehensive that its many parts need to be taught with emphasis and clarity. It inspires unlimited thousands of messages. As the title of our book suggests, there are two literal, invisible kingdoms operating at the same time and in the same place, at war with each other. Both seek the loyalty of humans. While the Holy Bible describes them, we confirm them with on-going evidence and testimonies that prove the Bible is the ultimate authority. Apart from it I have nothing to offer.

7. Many people regard all of this as science fiction. What would you say to them?

Answer: Yes, you are right. That is exactly what I thought at first. As it turns out, however, science fiction actually originates out of the Bible's description of the two literal, invisible kingdoms at war with each other. The remarkable thing is where you find them. Jesus explained that "The kingdom of God is within you" (Luke 17:21). Now don't get mad when I tell you that the other kingdom is there also! The character and symptoms of both are described in the fifth chapter of Galatians. Verses 17-21describe the evil, and verses 22 through 26 describe the righteous. Our trilogy of books expands upon these terse facts in cryptic detail to show readers how to be victorious "... over all the power of the devil "(Luke 10:19).

8. Why does it take three books to cover one subject?

Answer: Actually, all of them were written to be one manuscript for a single volume. But editor, Terry Lea, decided it covered too much for only one, so she broke it into three. I guess she thought

I was "the man who wrote too much". While she edited, I kept on writing, until she urged me to "stop writing!" Her assessment was correct. It takes a lot to convince folks to believe what seems unbelievable. It is a stretch for them to believe that battles are waged first inside the mind before they destroy the body through disease, calamity, and death.

9. Would you classify this as a book of theology? What practical use does it have?

Answer: It is a small but important fraction of what Jesus taught, and theological only in the sense of practical, miraculous demonstrations. He healed the sick, raised the dead, opened blind eyes, and cast out demons. This book teaches the same things using Jesus' own words but expands upon a side of spiritual warfare that most have neglected to teach. It is practical in showing others how to do the same things one-on-one that Jesus did. It does not discuss miraculous so much as it is miraculous. It also is prophecy, and history of the past, present, and the future, presenting little talk and much action.

10. What type of feedback have you had from readers?

Answer: Three features have been most talked about. First were comments like, "It's scary". I told them "I guarantee that if you read the first 50 pages you will be delivered from the spirit of fear. That deliverance actually occurred for several merely by reading them.

Second, the most popular segment has been the Warfare Decree. Several readers told me they declared the decree in their residence, and that doing so chased away the gloom they had experienced. Their residence was delivered or freed from resident evil spirits.

Third, readers said they had to read various sections several times to comprehend the startling revelations presented.

Fourth, it became apparent that negative emotions and destructive behaviors often originated through the work of demons, as confirmed by the Scriptures.

11. That's an amazing set of claims.

Answer: Yes, much as the claims of Jesus' personal ministry were amazing and true.

12. Where is your book offered for sale?

Answer: Wherever books in print are sold. Amazon is the primary distributor both online and in store.

Revelation 7:12 "...Blessing, and glory, and wisdom, and thanksgiving, and honour, and power, and might, be unto our God forever and ever. Amen. "

RECOMMENDED DELIVERANCE RESOURCES

DEREK PRINCE MINISTRIES
P.O. BOX 19501
Charlotte, NC 28219 www.derekprince.org/fyp
Phone: 1-800-448-3281
50 books written by Derek Prince.
Cassettes, CD's, DVD's, Streaming, mp3.
Brilliant teaching on most Bible subjects.
Pioneer in deliverance.

IMPACT CHRISTIAN BOOKS
332 Leffingwell Ave.
Kirkwood, MO 63122
www.impactchristianbooks.com
Phone: 1-800-451-2708 or 1-314-822-3309
Publisher, bookstore, distributor.
Books, DVD's. Broad subject variety.
Many titles on the subject of deliverance.

LAKE HAMILTON BIBLE CAMP
Merrill Miller
P.O. Box 21516
Hot Springs, AR 71903
www.lakehamiltonbiblecamp.com
lhbconline.com
e-mail: 72LHBC@cablelynx.com
Quarterly deliverance camp meetings.
Books, DVD's. Specialize in deliverance.

RECOMMENDED COMPANION BOOKS
War on the Saints - by Jesse Penn-Lewis
Pigs in the Parlor - by Frank Hammond
War in Heaven - by Derek Prince
Annihilating the Hosts of Hell - by Win Worley
Stronger Than Satan - Dr. John Polis

DELIVERANCE THEME BOOK TRILOGY
Book One: War of the World, Flesh, and the Devil
Book Two: Liberation of Mind, Will, and Intellect
Book Three: Restoration of Spirit, Soul, and Body

License to republish in national languages may be available under contract for single book title or for the trilogy of books – print, e-book, or both. For information, contact publisher or author.

Looking for a professional book designer?

Let's talk!

Sally Edens
Graphic & Website Designer
918.280.9167
www.mycreativepixel.com
@mycreativepixel

With B&B Publishing you will receive one on one interaction and a quality product you will be happy to show your friends.

Beth Mayer | 843-929-8768 | BandBpublishingLLC.com